KT-104-720

FIRST WORLD WAR
...CORDS

A Gui... ...amily Historians

57 148 613

FIRST WORLD WAR ARMY SERVICE RECORDS

A Guide for Family Historians

William Spencer

The National Archives

First published in 2008 by
The National Archives
Kew, Richmond
Surrey TW9 4DU
United Kingdom

www.nationalarchives.gov.uk

The National Archives brings together the Public
Record Office, Historical Manuscripts Commission,
Office of Public Sector Information and Her Majesty's
Stationery Office.

© Text copyright William Spencer 2008

The right of William Spencer to be identified as the
Author of this work has been asserted by him in
accordance with the Copyright, Designs and Patents
Act 1988.

All rights reserved. No part of this publication may be
reproduced, stored in a retrieval system or transmitted,
in any form or by any means, electronic, mechanical,
photocopying, recording or otherwise without the
prior permission of both the copyright holder and the
above publisher.

A catalogue card for this book is available from
the British Library.

ISBN 978 1 905615 26 1

Jacket and typographic design by
Ken Wilson | point 918
Typesetting by Goldust Design

Printed in Great Britain by
The Cromwell Press Ltd., Trowbridge, Wiltshire

COVER IMAGES: (centre) British troops boarding
London omnibuses at Arras on their return from the
capture of Monchy-le-Preux by men of the 37th
Division at the Battle of the Scarpe, April 1917.
(Photograph Q 06228 courtesy of the Imperial War
Museum, London)
(top) Troops of the 3rd Battalion, Royal Fusiliers,
manning a trench near Bairakli Jum'a, Salonika, 1917.
(Photograph Q 32896 courtesy of the Imperial War
Museum, London)

FRONTISPIECE: British troops moving from a reserve
trench to the front line near Tilloy-les-Mofflaines during
the Battle of Arras. (Photograph Q 1995 courtesy of the
Imperial War Museum, London).

PICTURE CREDITS: The Silver War Badge (Fig. 30)
appears courtesy of the author.
Images in the text: Figs 15 (Q 15597), 19 (HU 63277B),
20 (HU 81079), 45 (CO 997), 46 (E[AUS] 19), 47 (Q
104057), 49 (Q 2031), 50 (Q 1995) and 54 (Q 4012)
appear courtesy of the Imperial War Museum, London.
The rest of the images in this book are taken from the
files of the National Archives and, unless otherwise
mentioned, are © Crown copyright.

ACKNOWLEDGEMENTS

I would like to thank the following people for
their help in producing this work: my
colleagues in The National Archives, especially
Catherine Bradley, publisher, my ever-patient
editor Janet Sacks, Hugh Alexander, Brian
Carter and Paul Johnson of the Image Library;
and friends and contacts David Lloyd, Paul
Baillie, Dave Morris, Tony Farrington and
Keith Steward.

My final thanks as always go to Kate,
Lucy and Alice for allowing me to prepare this
book and once again neglect my duties as a
husband and father, and to scatter papers
all over the house.

Marston's Pedigree still works!

WILLIAM SPENCER

CALDERDALE LIBRARIES	
Bertrams	31/07/2008
940.4094SP	£12.99
ML	L2067

CONTENTS

USING THE NATIONAL ARCHIVES

The National Archives is the national repository for government records in the UK. Its main site at Kew holds the surviving records of government back to the Domesday Book (1086) and beyond. It is the best place to search for an ancestor in the armed forces.

Most of the records described in this guide can be consulted at The National Archives, Ruskin Avenue, Kew, Richmond, Surrey, TW9 4DU. The Archives are open 09:00–17:00 on Mondays and Fridays, 09:00–19:00 on Tuesdays and Thursdays, 10:00–17:00 on Wednesdays and 09:30–17:00 on Saturdays. They are closed on Sundays, public holidays, and for annual stocktaking. The website address is:

www.nationalarchives.gov.uk

The Archives are about 10 minutes' walk from Kew Gardens Underground Station, which is on London Transport's District Line, as well as the London Overground Service. For motorists, it is just off the South Circular Road (A205). There is adequate parking.

The National Archives can be a confusing place to use. If you are new to researching there, it is a good idea to allow plenty of time to find your feet. The staff are both knowledgeable and friendly, and are happy to help if you get lost. There is a public restaurant and a well-stocked bookshop on site. Self-service lockers are available to store your belongings.

Accessing the records is simple. First you need to obtain a reader's ticket, which is free, when you arrive. Please bring two forms of identity, such as a passport or driving licence, and something with an address, such as a utility bill or bank statement. If you are not a British citizen, you will need your passport. For further information see:

www.nationalarchives.gov.uk/visit/whattobring.htm

It is possible to get photocopies and/or digital copies of most documents you find: please ask the staff for details. It is also possible for you to use your own digital camera to copy documents.

In order to protect the documents, each one of which is unique, security in the reading rooms is tight. You are only permitted to take a camera, laptop, notebook and notes into the reading rooms and can only use a pencil. Eating and drinking are not permitted in the reading rooms.

The records held by the National Archives are described and ordered using a three-part reference. The first element is known as the 'department' and takes the form of letters. The 'department' denotes which government department created the records. The second element is known as the 'series' and collects together records of a similar type. The second element is in the form of numbers. The third and final element of a document reference is known as the 'piece' and this usually is just a number, but occasionally may include letters.

Over time, terminology used to describe the document references at the National Archives has changed and you may hear terms such as 'letter codes' and 'class' still being used. Letter codes are, of course, the 'department' and 'class' is the 'series'. Whilst such terminology is interchangeable, many of the 'department' identities, irrespective of whether they are being called 'department' or 'letter code', are obvious, with WO being the War Office, ADM being the Admiralty and AIR being the Air Ministry. Other 'department' identities are not so obvious; the records of MI5, for example, are identified by the letters KV (it's an anagram of significance for you to work out) and the Welsh Office uses BD. Most unit war diaries for the First World War are, for example, in the series WO 95. It is these department and series references that are referred to throughout this guide.

Brief descriptions of every document ('piece' is the term used by the National Archives) are in the series lists. Several sets of lists are available in the Open Reading Room and other locations. The series list gives you the exact reference of the document you want. This is what you order on the computer terminal. Occasionally in this guide we use the full reference, written thus: WO 95/898.

An increasing number of documents are available on microfilm, microfiche or in digitized format. Where this is the case, the fact is noted in the text. You do not need to order microfilms on the computer as you can help yourself to them in the Open Reading Room.

In addition, there are various other finding aids for genealogists. The best general overview is provided by Amanda Bevan's revised *Tracing Your Ancestors in The National Archives* (7th edition, TNA, 2006).

The structure and development of the War Office is fully described in Michael Roper's handbook *The Records of the War Office and related departments, 1660–1964.*

The National Archives Online

As well as giving information on where the National Archives is, opening times and how to gain access, the National Archives website gives details about popular records, including research guides and lists of independent researchers. Most importantly, the website allows readers to access the National Archives Catalogue (series lists).

The Catalogue can be searched by using keywords, dates and, if you know them, the department (letter code) and series (class) where records are known to exist.

Follow these simple steps to identify the documents you require:

1. Locate the Catalogue.
2. Click on *Search the Catalogue*.
3. Type in keyword(s) into the top box, the year range (as appropriate) into the two boxes below the keyword box and, if known, the departmental code and series (optional) into the last (bottom) box.
4. It is possible to use more than one keyword, either by just putting the words in or by doing a combined word search linking the words together with AND.
5. Click on *Search*.

The computer will then search for documents of interest that include the search term(s) you used and that are included in a document description. Document descriptions and the references under which they will need to be ordered will be listed as either individual items or, in the case of multiple results, under the department code (the letters) and then with the number of results in blue at the right-hand side. Click on the blue number to obtain more detailed descriptions of these results.

Many records have been or are in the process of being digitized and placed on the DocumentsOnline section of the National Archives website. Among these records are the First World War Army medal index cards (WO 372), some of the unit war diaries in WO 95, the Women's Royal Air Force records of service (AIR 80) and the Women's Army Auxiliary Corps records of service (WO 398). In each case it is possible to search these records by name and, where appropriate, to download them for a fee.

This document records that

L/Sgt J W Stones of the
19th Battalion, The Durham Light Infantry

who was executed for casting away arms on
18 January 1917 is pardoned under Section
359 of the Armed Forces Act 2006.

The pardon stands as recognition that he was
one of many victims of the First World War
and that execution was not a fate he deserved.

Secretary of State for Defence

INTRODUCTION

As we fast approach the centenary of the outbreak of the First World War, interest in its participants and events continues to increase. The National Archives, with its celebrated collection of First World War material — from the service records of thousands of soldiers to details of campaign medals and meritorious service awards, courts martial and casualty lists—is a major source for anyone exploring the conflict. It holds records on Dominion Forces and the Indian Army, the WAAC, the Royal Flying Corps and RAF, nursing and auxilliary services. Yet despite the range of original documents now available, until the Ministry of Defence (Army) releases the remaining records of service for personnel who served in the First World War and beyond, the study of those who took part in the war cannot be complete.

Ninety years have now passed since the guns fell silent on the Western Front, but events in parts of the world today can be compared to those experienced by many First World War service personnel. Operations in Mesopotamia and Iraq in 1919 and 1920, and in Afghanistan in 1919, and current operations in Iraq (Operation Telic) and Afghanistan (Operation Herrick) are two examples. The only thing that has changed dramatically for the fighting man on the ground today compared with 90 years ago is the technology — the terrain and enemy have changed very little!

In the seven years since the last edition of this work, the number of records being made available has not changed much—but the means of accessing them has. This fourth edition both highlights new record releases and shows how to get the most out of new forms of document delivery, such as digitized records and access via the internet. Digitized records are now easily accessible via a computer, whereas in the past they could be seen only by those able to visit Kew in southwest London. Men and women of the British Army of the First World War period settled in several different countries after 1918, and in many cases it is their children and grandchildren who are now accessing their ancestors' records from Australia, Canada, New Zealand and South Africa.

Fig. 1 *Pardon notice placed in the courts martial proceedings of all those soldiers pardoned for committing military offences during the war.* WO 71/535

The most noticeable change for the First World War researcher of today compared with seven years ago is thus the use of technology. While not everything is available at the click of a button, the most important information is, at least for other ranks. This includes the records of service in WO 363 and WO 364, the medal records in WO 372 and the operational records in WO 95. Improvements to the cataloguing of officers' records of service may one day mean that a computer and credit card may be all that you need to research a serviceman or woman of the First World War!

The records of the First World War are not just for the family or military historian — local, medical and legal historians, for example, all use the records. The local historian researches the names from their war memorial, the medical historian looks at how warfare changed medicine and how certain injuries and illnesses were treated, and the legal historian is interested in how the Army punished its wrongdoers, as well as how they made mistakes and learned from some of them. The current British Army has used First World War records to see how the Army learned about mountain warfare in 1917 and 1918.

This guide is designed to help anyone with an interest in the men and women of the First World War to find out something about them — when they served, where they served, where they fought and died, where they are buried or commemorated, what medals they were awarded, and much more. Their courage and resilience deserves to be celebrated, and by discovering real information about real people, we are helping to keep the memory of those caught up in 'the war to end all wars' alive.

WILLIAM SPENCER

CALDERDALE LIBRARIES

1 RECORDS OF THOSE WHO SERVED IN THE FIRST WORLD WAR

Researchers who are looking for information about an individual who served in the war frequently ask: 'How many people served in the First World War and how many records does the National Archives hold?'

The answer to the first part of this question is that over eight million men and women saw service in the British forces between 1914 and 1918. At the outbreak of war the Army numbered 733,514 men. By the end of the war 7,712,772 men and women had enlisted. The Royal Flying Corps (RFC) numbered only 1,900 men but by the end of the war 293,522 had enlisted in the RFC and Royal Air Force (RAF). The total naval enlistments numbered 407,360. Altogether, the total number of men and women who enlisted and saw service in the British armed forces between 1914 and 1918 was 9,296,691.

The number of enlistments during the war can be found in *Statistics of Military Effort of the British Empire during the Great War*. However, to place the records and the men and women who can be found in them into some sort of perspective it is worth noting the following:

Strength of British Army (Regulars), Territorial Force and Reservists as at August 1914	733,514
Enlistments August 1914–December 1915	2,466,719

Without adding the remaining enlistments for the rest of the war to these figures, this number has already exceeded the total number of records of service held in WO 339, WO 363, WO 364 and WO 374.

The second part of the question is a little more difficult to answer. Whilst the records discussed in this guide certainly number in the millions, an accurate total of surviving First World War records may never be known. There are a number of reasons for this uncertainty.

The most significant reason is the Arnside Street fire on 8 September 1940. Arnside Street was the location of the War Office records repository and in it were housed various records of those personnel who had seen service in the First World War. The majority of the records housed in the repository were either totally destroyed or

SECRET

G.H.Q. 66.

Copy No. 20

FOURTH ARMY OPERATION ORDER NO. 2.

(Reference map issued with G.X.3/1.P dated 5th June, 1916).

1. The Fourth Army will take part in a general offensive with a view to breaking up the enemy's defensive system and of exploiting to the full all opportunities opened up for defeating his forces within reach.

2. The Third, First and Second Armies are undertaking offensive operations at various points along their fronts in conformity with the attack of the Fourth Army.

The objectives of the Third Army will include an attack on GOMMECOURT, which will be simultaneous with the attack of the Fourth Army.

3. The French will assume the offensive on both banks of the SOMME. The XX French Corps, in close touch with the right of the Fourth Army, is attacking at the same hour North of the SOMME.

4. The three successive tasks of the Fourth Army are:-

(1) To capture the enemy's defences on the line MONTAUBAN - POZIERES - SERRE, forming a strong defensive flank on the GRANDCOURT - SERRE Ridge.

(2) To extend the defensive flank from GRANDCOURT to MARTINPUICH, and, at the same time, advance our line eastward to the line MONTAUBAN - MARTINPUICH.

(3) To attack eastward from the line MONTAUBAN - MARTINPUICH and secure the BAZENTIN-le-GRAND - GINCHY plateau

The operations of the Fourth Army will be divided into phases as outlined above.

5. The first day's operations will include the capture and consolidation of MONTAUBAN, CONTALMAISON, POZIERES and SERRE, as indicated generally by the green line on the map.

As soon as this line has been gained and consolidated, preparations will immediately be undertaken to commence the second phase of the operations, the objectives of which are shewn generally by the brown line on the map.

The Army Commander wishes to impress on all commanders that the success of the operations as a whole largely depends on the consolidation of the definite objectives which have been allotted to each Corps. Beyond these objectives no serious advance is to be made until preparations have been completed for entering on the next phase of the operations.

/ 6.

Fig. 2 *Fourth Army operation order for the first day of the Battle of the Somme, 1 July 1916.* WO 158/234

badly damaged by fire and water. All those that survived the fire are preserved at the National Archives.

The second reason for the uncertainty is duplication. Although there are some 16 series containing records of service that date from the First World War period, many men and women had service files held by more than one government department and many of these duplicates have been preserved either in a WO record series or a PIN record series.

From the seven million-plus enlistments for all services must be taken the records of those who saw any service after 1920 as an other rank, or after March 1922 as an officer. This includes those whose service ended within the above prescribed dates but who were recalled or re-enlisted for service in the Second World War. These records are still maintained by the Ministry of Defence.

1.1 Why the records are as they are

Information regarding the physical structure and state of the officers' records are discussed elsewhere (see chapter 2). As a greater percentage of surviving records are for officers, you are more likely to find a record for an officer than for an other rank. However, it is the records of the other ranks that generate the most interest and the most questions.

No one knows how the War Office record repository on Arnside Street was laid out. However, there are a number of theories. As the records of service were originally held at regional record offices (see Appendix 2), it would seem logical that the records could have been kept in these collections. Therefore the arrangement may have been by record office first and then by regiment/corps.

Due to the way the Army expanded during the war, the arrangement of the records of service for each regiment/corps was probably in alphabetical order, with the common names perhaps in regimental number order. Since a given regiment/corps was made up of men from the Regular Army, territorial force and conscripts, many of whom served in what in reality were either regular, territorial or service battalions, for example, it would have been time-consuming and impractical to separate their records of service into these categories. Until a complete survey of the surviving soldiers' records is completed, which units personnel records are there and which are not will remain subject to speculation. However, by using the record office data in Appendix 2 and by searching for records on *www.ancestry.co.uk* by regiment, a better understanding of the surviving records of service may be achieved.

Fig. 3, 4 (overleaf and following page) *A rare example of an Army Form B 199A, and an officer's record of service. The majority of such forms were destroyed by enemy action in 1940.* WO 374/1881

(1 9 70) W2005—PP2701 50,000 1/19 HWV(R439)
Number of Personal Paper.

Army Form B. 199A.

Serial Number on Index Card. 3303

Regiment or Corps. *Royal Garrison Artillery* (91878) RE/2145   Surname. ANLEY.

Christian Names. WILLIAM BOWER.   Initials. W.B.A.   (Title, if any). nil

(1.) WHERE EDUCATED	(a) Schools *Royal Naval Academy, Gosport.*	Date of Birth 23rd May 1871.	Officer *British*
	(b) University —	Place of Birth *Binstead, Ryde, I.O.W.* NATIONALITY OR	Officer's Father *British*
	or Technical College —	Religious Denomination *C & E.*	Mother *British*

(2.) Name and Address of Next-of-kin or Guardian, other than Wife (for reference in case of emergency)

	Relationship	Name and Address of Bankers or Agents
Mrs. H.T. ANLEY. BINSTEAD RYDE ISLE OF WIGHT.	MOTHER.	Messrs COX & COY. Charing Cross London

(3.)

If Married, Name of Wife	Date of Marriage	Names of Children living	Date of Birth	Sex
No	—	—	—	—

(4.) Schools and Courses of Instruction	Place	Year	Result	Authority
Short Course of Gunnery	Shoebury	1891	—	
Long Course of Gunnery	Woolwich & Shoebury	1896	1st Class with Horses	

(5.) Staff College Exams.	Place	Date	Authority
(a) If passed Staff College ...	No		
(b) If qualified for Staff College without obtaining vacancy, giving date...	No		
(c) If entered for Staff College Exam., but failed, giving date ...	No		

(6.) Examination for Promotion	Date	Special Certificate	Failed
LIEUTENANT...	Nov 1899		No
CAPTAIN	1900	Yes - & D in 3 Subjects	No
MAJOR	—	—	No
LIEUT.-COLONEL	—	—	No

(7.) SPECIAL QUALIFICATIONS

(a) Foreign Languages ...   nil

(b) Knowledge of Foreign Countries   nil

(c) Business Qualifications ...   nil

(d) Legal Qualifications (giving particulars) ... ...   nil

(e) Professional or Artistic qualifications or degrees, or Membership, etc., of Learned Society ... ...   nil

(f) Any special knowledge or experience not included in (a) to (e)   nil

(8.)

Campaigns	Period From	To	(10.) Honours and Rewards, including Mentions in Despatches	Date of Gazette or other Authority
Operations in France & Belgium	Feby 1916	Nov 1919	Mention	Dec 1916
			D.S.O	1.1.17.
			Mention	June 1917
			Belgium Croix de Guerre	Jany 1918.

(9.)

Wounds and Nature	Place and Date	Pension or Gratuity
nil	—	—

Particulars of Service, Record of Movements, Appointments, Promotions, Etc.	Station	Date	Authority	Service At Home	Service Abroad	
3rd Royal Guernsey Militia	Guernsey	Early 1889		3/12 (about)		Preliminary Training
Royal Military Academy	Woolwich	Jan: 1889		2 6/12		
First Commission as Lieutenant		24.7.91	L. Gazette			
Short Course of Gunnery	Shoebury	Sept 1891		3/12		
14 Company Southern Division Royal Artillery	Weymouth	1891		3 & 2/12		
Long Course of Gunnery	Woolwich & Shoebury	} 1893-5		1		Still belonging to 14 Coy SD RA.
14 Company Southern Division Royal Artillery	Portsmouth	1895		1 8/12		
Officer ic Danger Buildings Waltham Abbey	Waltham Abbey	1897		4 6/12		
Promoted Captain		Nov: 1899	L. Gazette			
33rd Battalion Imperial Yeomanry	Aldershot & South Africa	} April 1902		1/12	9/12	
100 Company R.G.A.	Gibraltar	April 1903			7/12	
Adjutant R.A. Ceylon	Colombo	Nov 1903			3 6/12	
30 Company R.G.A.	Weymouth	May 1907		3		
87 Company R.G.A.	Hong Kong	Oct 1910			1	
Promoted Major		11.10.11	L. Gazette			
Armament Major	Singapore	Dec 1911		1	1	
2nd Depot R.G.A.	Yarmouth	Jan 1914		1 3/12		
131 Heavy Battery R.G.A.	Woolwich	Dec 1915		2/12		
40 Siege Battery R.G.A.	Plymouth, Lydd, Portsmouth & France	} May 1915		9/12	3/12	
Acting Lieut. Colonel		July 1916	L. Gazette			
39 Group R.G.A.	France	July 1916			7/12	
Counter Battery Staff Officer attached VII Corps R.A.	France	Feb 1917			1 9/12	
Promoted Lieut: Colonel		1.5.17	L. Gazette			
Brigadier General VII Corps Heavy Artillery		8.11.18	L. Gazette			
Commanding VII Corps Heavy Artillery	France	8.11.18			8/12	Still serving as such. —

Finding of Medical Boards	Date	Nature of Disability	Place where held and Authority	Sick Leave Granted From	To
Fit for Foreign Service	1905	Eczema	(1) Ceylon (2) Portsmouth	6 months	
	1911		(3) Hong Kong	6 months	
Fit for Foreign Service.	1912		(4) Portsmouth		
3 months light duty at home	1914	Appendicitis	(5) Yarmouth	nil	

In order to supplement the surviving records and to replace those lost in 1940, the War Office, at the end of the Second World War, made an appeal to those other government departments that might have held records of service to return them to the War Office. The Ministry of Pensions returned the largest collection, which related to men who had been discharged from the Army suffering from either wounds or sickness. These records are in WO 364. The arrangement of all of the records at that time is unknown. However, all of the surviving records were put into alphabetical sequences after the Second World War. The 'Burnt' records are in WO 363 and the 'Unburnt' records, already mentioned, are in WO 364.

The surviving other ranks' records of service are held in some 44,000 boxes. As the collection is so big and the majority of it is too delicate to be handled, the records have been made available on microfilm with the help of the Heritage Lottery Fund. By the time the project finished in the summer of 2002, over 15,000 reels of microfilm were produced, preserving the military careers of some 2.8 million individuals. Added to the 217,737 officers' files this will mean that some three million records documenting Army personnel of the First World War will be available for all to see.

2 OFFICERS' RECORDS OF SERVICE

Prior to the outbreak of the First World War, there were approximately 15,000 officers holding commissions. During the period of hostilities another 235,000 individuals were granted either temporary or permanent commissions in the British Army.

From a total of some 250,000 officers who held a commission at any time between 1914 and 1918, the records of some individuals are not available. Officers who were still serving after 31 March 1922 or who had left the Army prior to that date but rejoined or were recalled for further service, for example in the Second World War, have files still retained by the Ministry of Defence. In most cases the files retained can be identified by the presence of a 'P' number file reference alongside the officers' names in WO 338. The 'P' or 'Personal' file system replaced all of the other officers' file references that had been used during the war. This new file system started on 1 April 1922 and, apart from the exceptional cases where files may be found, for example in WO 138 (see 2.5.4), all of the surviving 'P' files are with the Ministry of Defence.

The two main record series containing records of service of officers who saw service in the First World War represent the careers of some 217,000 individuals. Amongst these files can be found many well-known names, some famous for their service during the war, others for something they did before or after the war. They are all there for you to discover.

Originally an officer's file consisted of three main parts; the record of service in the form of the Army Form B 199 (AF B 199), the confidential reports in the Army Form B 196 and the correspondence file. In all but the rarest of cases, only the correspondence file has survived.

The AF B 199 was a single sheet, completed on both sides, which contained most of the relevant data about an officer, including his biographical details, qualifications, courses he had attended, details about active service and any awards he received. The information on the forms was entered as events occurred. As they would appear rather untidy, with lots of different styles of writing on them, the

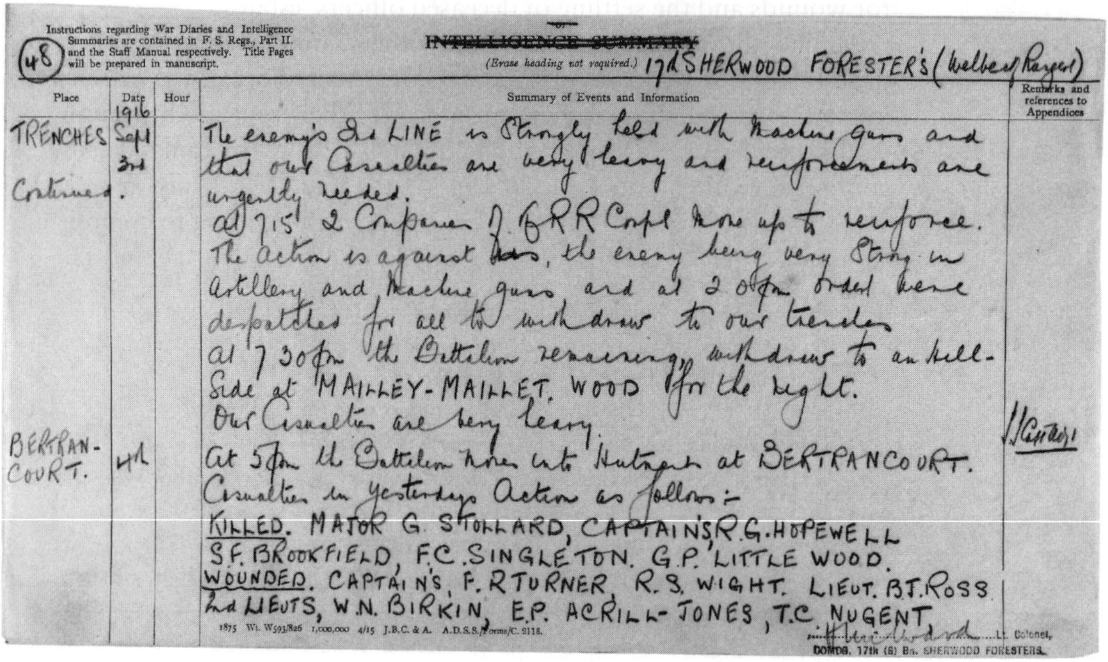

Fig. 5 *Unit war diary for 17 Battalion Sherwood Foresters (Welbeck Rangers), recording operations and casualties on the Somme in September 1916. WO 95/2587*

forms were renewed every five years, the entries being completed in one colour of ink, in one hand.

The reason for the lack of at least two parts of most officers' records of service can be explained. The AF B 199s for officers commissioned prior to 1901 may be found bound in Army Book 83s in WO 76. The confidential reports for officers of the same period no longer survive. The correspondence files for these men, in most cases, have not survived unless they were recalled for service during the First World War, having retired prior to 1914, or were still serving when war broke out. Even then in many cases files no longer exist.

The AF B 199s and AF B 196s for officers who were commissioned after 1901 were separated from the correspondence files and stored at the Arnside Street record repository, where they were destroyed in 1940. In between the extraction of these parts of the whole files, the remaining correspondence in each file underwent the usual record-keeping practice of being weeded of all unimportant material. It must be remembered that the War Office still had access to the two parts of the file it had removed and therefore only kept that type of information that was not kept on an AF B 199 or AF B 196. The consequence of standard archival practice and the destruction of the more inform-ative parts of most officers' files in 1940, is that all that survives may seem very bland and uninformative — but there is a reason for it. What remains relates primarily to money, length of service, pensions

20 · *Officers' Records of Service*

for wounds and the settling of deceased officers' estates.

Unlike the records of service of other ranks, where there can usually be found a collection of standard Army Forms, the officers' files vary according to the circumstances of their route to a commission. The files of those officers commissioned from the ranks usually contain the other ranks' records of service and their Army Form B 103 Casualty Form—Active service. Initial forms relating to commissions come in four main types (examples are shown in Figs. 9 and 10):

Army Form B 201. Application for Appointment to the Special Reserve of Officers

Army Form MT 939. Application for Appointment to a Temporary Commission in the Regular Army for the Period of the War

Army Form W 3361. Notification of Posting on First Appointment

For Officers commissioned prior to August 1914. A Form of Particulars: Examination for Admission to the Royal Military Academy Sandhurst or Royal Military College Woolwich

2.1 Types of Commissions

During the First World War there were different types of commission depending on the status of the unit in which a man served or the preference of the individual being commissioned.

Those officers who were holding commissions prior to the outbreak of the war held either permanent commissions in the Regular Army, territorial commissions or commissions in the reserve of officers. The officers who were holding Territorial Army commissions at the outbreak of the war could originally have held a commission in the Militia, Special Reserve, Yeomanry or Volunteers. These commissions are in parts of the Army that were united into the Territorial Force (later Army) upon its creation in 1908.

Officers commissioned during the war were usually granted temporary commissions, in either the Regular Army, the Territorial Force (later Army) or the Special Reserve of Officers. A small number of officers were granted permanent commissions in the Regular Army.

In most cases it is possible to tell what type of commission had been granted to an officer by consulting the *Army List*. In the name index of the *Army List* letters are used to signify the part of the Army into which an officer had been commissioned:

M   Militia
R   Special Reserve of Officers
T   Territorial Force
V   Volunteers
Y   Yeomanry

If there is no prefix alongside the name of an officer then he was commissioned into the Regular Army.

For more information on the *Army List* see 2.6.

2.2 WO 338

WO 338 is the name index for the records preserved in WO 339 (see 2.2.1) and provides the all-important 'Long Number' which needs to be obtained in order that the file can be identified in WO 339. The indexes in WO 338 consist of 24 pieces, all of which are available on microfilm. WO 338/1–21 is the name index for officers commissioned between 1901 and 1922. WO 338/22 is the index of officers commissioned between 1870 and 1901. WO 338/23 is the index of officers of the Royal Army Medical Corps (RAMC) commissioned between 1871 and 1921, but does not include the temporary officers mentioned below in 2.4.

LIST OF WO 338 INDEXES

WO 338	Date Range	Surnames
1	1901–22	A
2	1901–22	Ba–Bl
3	1901–22	Bo–By
4	1901–22	Ca–Cl
5	1901–22	Co–Cz
6	1901–22	D
7	1901–22	E–F
8	1901–22	G
9	1901–22	Ha–Hep
10	1901–22	Her–Hy
11	1901–22	I–K
12	1901–22	L
13	1901–22	Ma–Michaelson
14	1901–22	Micholson–O
15	1901–22	P
16	1901–22	Q–R
17	1901–22	Sa–Smith, George
18	1901–22	Smith, Gerald–Sz
19	1901–22	T–V
20	1901–22	Wa–Wilber
21	1901–22	Wilberforce–Z
22	1870–1901	Old Numbers A–Z
23	1871–1921	Medical Officers A–Z

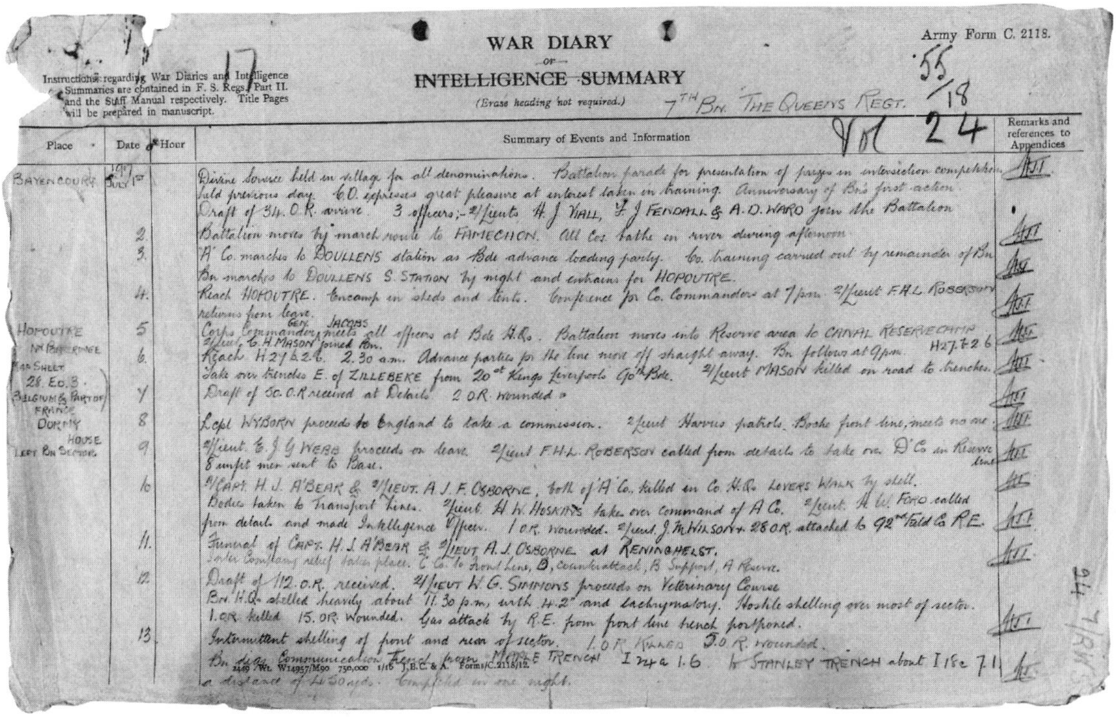
WAR DIARY
or
INTELLIGENCE SUMMARY
(Erase heading not required.)
Army Form C. 2118.
Instructions regarding War Diaries and Intelligence Summaries are contained in F. S. Regs. Part II. and the Staff Manual respectively. Title Pages will be prepared in manuscript.
7TH BN. THE QUEENS REGT.
Vol 24

Place	Date	Hour	Summary of Events and Information	Remarks and references to Appendices
BAYENCOURT	1917 July 1st		Divine Service held in village for all denominations. Battalion parade for presentation of prizes in inter-section competition held previous day. C.O. expresses great pleasure at interest taken in training. Anniversary of Bn's first action. Draft of 34. O.R. arrive. 3 officers;- 2/Lieuts H. J. VIALL, F. J. FENDALL & A. D. WARD join the Battalion	
	2.		Battalion moves by march route to FAMECHON. All Cos bathe in river during afternoon	
	3.		'A' Co. marches to DOULLENS station as Bde advance loading party. Co. training carried out by remainder of Bn. Bn marches to DOULLENS S. STATION by night and entrains for HOPOUTRE.	
	4.		Reach HOPOUTRE. Encamp in sheds and tents. Conference for Co. Commanders at 7 pm. 2/Lieut F. H. L. ROBERSON returns from leave.	
HOPOUTRE	5		Corps Commander Gen. JACOBS meets all officers at Bde H.Q. Battalion moves into Reserve area to CANAL RESERVE CAMP. 2/Lieut. C. H. MASON joined Bn.	
Nr BUSSEBOOM	6.		Reach H27 b 2.6. 2.30 a.m. Advance parties for the line move off straight away. Bn follows at 9 pm. Take over trenches E. of ZILLEBEKE from 20th Kings Liverpools 30th Bde. 2/Lieut MASON killed on road to trenches.	H27.7.2 6
Map Sheet 28. Ed. 3. Belgium & Part of France	7		Draft of 50. O.R. received at Details. 2 O.R. wounded.	
DORMY HOUSE	8		Lcpl WYBORN proceeds to England to take a commission. 2/Lieut Harris patrols Boche front line, meets no one.	
Left Bn Sector	9		2/Lieut. E. J. G. WEBB proceeds on leave. 2/Lieut F. H. L. ROBERSON called from details to take over 'D' Co in Reserve line. 8 unfit men sent to Base.	
	10		A/Capt. H. J. A'BEAR & 2/Lieut. A. J. F. OSBORNE, both of 'A' Co. killed in Co. H.Q. LOVERS WALK by shell. Bodies taken to Transport Lines. 2/Lieut. H. W. HOSKINS take over command of A Co. 2/Lieut. A. W. FORD called from details and made Intelligence Officer. 1 O.R. wounded. 2/Lieut. J. M. WILSON & 28 O.R. attached to 92nd Field Co R.E.	
	11.		Funeral of Capt. H. J. A'BEAR & 2/Lieut A. J. OSBORNE at RENINGHELST. Inter Company relief takes place. C Co. to front line, D, counterattack, B Support, A Reserve.	
	12.		Draft of 112. O.R. received. 2/Lieut W. G. SIMMONS proceeds on Veterinary Course. Bn. H.Q. shelled heavily about 11.30 p.m. with 4.2" and Lachrymatory. Hostile shelling over most of sector. 1. O.R. killed 15. O.R. wounded. Gas attack by R.E. from front line trench postponed.	
	13.		Intermittent shelling of front and rear of sector. 1. O.R. Killed 5. O.R. wounded. Bn dug Communication Trench from MAPLE TRENCH I 24 a 1.6 to STANLEY TRENCH about I 18 c 7.1 a distance of 450 yds. Completed in one night.	

2449 Wt. W14957/M90 750,000 1/16 J.B.C. & A. Forms/C.2118/12.

Fig. 6 *Unit war diary for 7 Battalion Queen's (Royal West Surrey) Regiment, recording Captain H. J. A'Bear's death on 10 July 1917.* WO 95/2051

The format of WO 338 is common to all pieces and the information is presented in six columns:

Surname	Initial(s)	Regt/Corps	Long Number	Rank	Remarks

Most of the information presented in the index is quite obvious. However, although the abbreviations used to denote the corps in which the officer was commissioned can easily be translated, the numerical codes used to identify infantry regiments are those used to identify the regiments prior to the 1881 Cardwell reforms. After 1881 regiments were known by name and not by their old numbers. The original numerical identity of infantry regiments can be found in Appendix 1. If the reference in the 'Long Number' column is made up of letters and numbers, usually the first letter of the surname and the first vowel of the surname, then this is a 'Vowel' reference. Files with 'Vowel' references are usually to be found in WO 374.

2.2.1 *WO 339*

The files preserved in WO 339 comprise the records of 139,906 officers who saw service during the First World War. The majority of the files are for officers for the duration of the war only: they were frequently referred to as 'Temporary Gentlemen' because they were

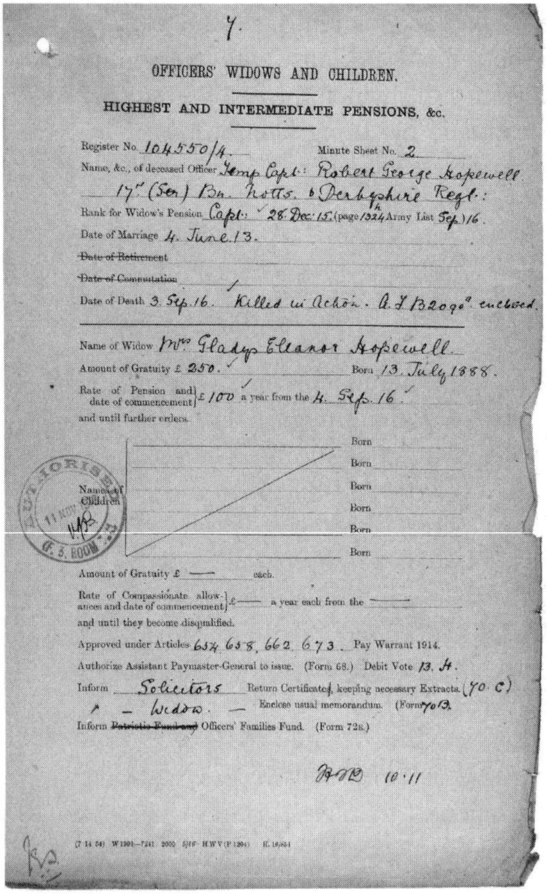

7.

OFFICERS' WIDOWS AND CHILDREN.

HIGHEST AND INTERMEDIATE PENSIONS, &c.

Register No. 104550/4. Minute Sheet No. 2

Name, &c., of deceased Officer Temp Capt: Robert George Hopewell 17th (Ser) Bn. Notts. & Derbyshire Regt:

Rank for Widow's Pension Capt: 28. Dec: 15. (page 1324 Army List Sep) 16.

Date of Marriage 4. June. 13.

~~Date of Retirement~~

~~Date of Commutation~~

Date of Death 3. Sep. 16. Killed in Action. A.F. B2090a enclosed.

Name of Widow Mrs Gladys Eleanor Hopewell.

Amount of Gratuity £ 250. Born 13. July 1888.

Rate of Pension and date of commencement £ 100 a year from the 4. Sep. 16.

and until further orders.

Names of Children — Born / Born / Born / Born / Born / Born

Amount of Gratuity £ — each.

Rate of Compassionate allowances and date of commencement £ — a year each from the —

and until they become disqualified.

Approved under Articles 654 658, 662 673. Pay Warrant 1914.

Authorize Assistant Paymaster-General to issue. (Form 68.) Debit Vote 13. H.

Inform Solicitors Return Certificates, keeping necessary Extracts. (70. C)

" — Widow. — Enclose usual memorandum. (Form 70 B.)

Inform ~~Patriotic Fund and~~ Officers' Families Fund. (Form 72a.)

AUTHORISED 11 NOV G. 5. ROOM

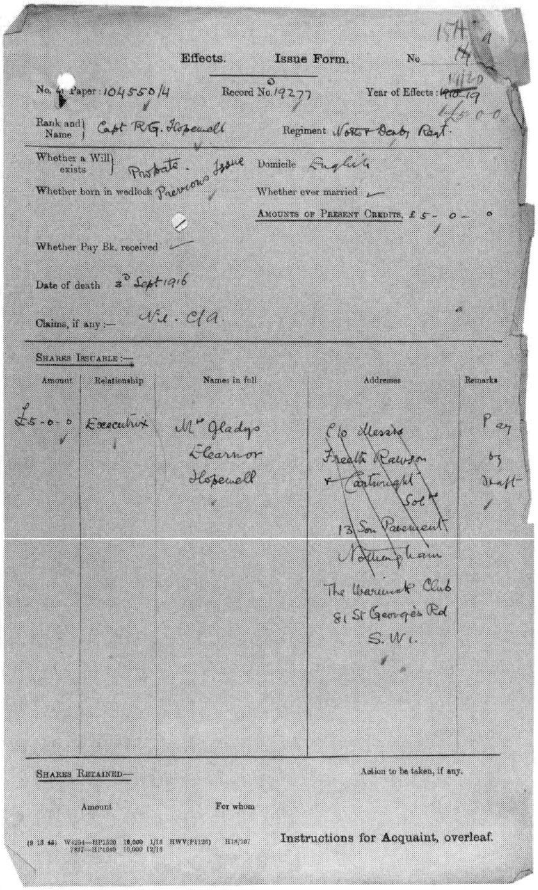

Effects. Issue Form. No. 14

No. of Paper: 104550/4 Record No. 19277 Year of Effects: 1918-19

Rank and Name: Capt R.G. Hopewell Regiment: Notts & Derby Regt.

Whether a Will exists: Probate. Previous Issue Domicile: English

Whether born in wedlock: Whether ever married: ✓

AMOUNTS OF PRESENT CREDITS. £ 5 – 0 – 0

Whether Pay Bk. received: —

Date of death: 3rd Sept 1916

Claims, if any: — Nil. C/a.

SHARES ISSUABLE:—

Amount	Relationship	Names in full	Addresses	Remarks
£5-0-0	Executrix	Mrs Gladys Eleanor Hopewell	~~C/o Messrs Freeth Rawson & Cartwright Sol[rs] 13 Low Pavement Nottingham~~ The Warwick Club 81 St George's Rd S.W.1.	Pay by Draft

SHARES RETAINED—

Amount / For whom

Action to be taken, if any.

Instructions for Acquaint, overleaf.

Fig. 7 (left) *Widow's Pension notification form for the widow of Captain R. G. Hopewell who was killed on 3 September 1916.* WO 339/37823

Fig. 8 (right) *Effects Issue Form of Captain R. G. Hopewell.* WO 339/37823

not considered to be of the right class. It is in this series that most of the officers who held Regular Army commissions and who were still serving at the outbreak of the war can be found, together with those granted emergency commissions in the Regular Army and those granted commissions in the Special Reserve of Officers. At the end of the WO 339 record series are a number of files for British Army other ranks who were commissioned into the Indian Army. See chapter 5 for further information.

What must be remembered when using WO 339 is that the content of the files is mostly correspondence relating to an officer and his service, rather than an operational record.

2.3 WO 374

The files preserved in WO 374 consist of the files of officers of the Territorial Force (later Army), a number of officers who came out of retirement, and other officers who do not really fit into either the Regular or Territorial Army; the civilian specialists who were granted commissions on account of certain skills which the Army needed.

Unlike WO 339, which is arranged by 'Long Number', WO 374 is arranged in alphabetical order, which includes all initials and rank (usually the highest confirmed rank an officer held).

2.4 Royal Army Medical Corps (Temporary) Commissions

During the First World War a large number of men with medical training was needed to cope with the high numbers of casualties. As a result of this, many doctors were granted temporary commissions in the Royal Army Medical Corps. As these officers were a discrete group, they were given their own series of records of service: the 24 Series. Unfortunately, as these RAMC (Temp) officers were only needed for the war, their records were all destroyed after 1920. Amongst these temporary officers whose records no longer exist are perhaps two of the most important doctors of the war: Noel Chavasse, VC and bar, MC, and James Churchill Dunn, DSO, MC, DCM, author of *The War the Infantry Knew*.

For an in-depth study of doctors in war, the problems relating to recruitment and the increasing need for more doctors due to the number of casualties and the diverse range of injuries, *Doctors in the Great War* by Ian R. Whitehead is the best book.

2.5 Other Record Series

There are a number of other record series that contain officers' records of service.

2.5.1 WO 25

In WO 25 there is a small collection of Royal Engineers officers' records, which are arranged by initial commission date. Although most of the volumes are pre-First World War, they do contain those pre-war officers and a number commissioned from the ranks in the early years of the war:

Reference	Date
WO 25/3913	1796–1860
WO 25/3914	1860–1921
WO 25/3915	1873–1928

WO 25/3916	1886–1918
WO 25/3917	1885–1937
WO 25/3918	1895–1935
WO 25/3919	1904–1915
WO 25/3920	1879–1915 (includes Supplementary Reserve)

2.5.2 *WO 76*

The surviving records of service for officers of the infantry and the cavalry, together with the Royal Engineers (Militia) officers, can be found in WO 76. These records date from the early nineteenth century to the First World War period and are arranged by record office and then by unit whose records were held by the particular record office.

The collection in WO 76 is, however, very inconsistent in both the date coverage and the units the record series covers. Whilst the complete series of records for the 1st battalion of a regiment may be found in WO 76, it is possible that the 2nd battalion may be missing, either in part or in total.

Records of the 3rd and 4th battalions of infantry regiments may also be found in WO 76.

2.5.3 *WO 68*

The records preserved in WO 68 consist of various types relating to the Militia. Arranged by unit, the records in this series include officers' records of service, bounty books for payments to other ranks, and records of units' services. Many of the records in WO 68 run up to the immediate pre-war period. Some include the period 1914–18. Further details about these records can be found in *Records of the Militia and Volunteer Forces 1757–1945* and *Army Records: A Guide for Family Historians*, both by William Spencer.

2.5.4 *WO 138*

The records of service preserved in the record series WO 138 may not be many but they are a very significant collection of officers' files covering the nineteenth and twentieth centuries. Amongst the files in this record series are a number of very important files belonging to officers who saw service in the First World War. Most of these files concern officers whose service led to an official War Office enquiry into their actions. The files of a number of officers who were sacked from an appointment during the war are preserved here, and the files not only contain their basic records of service but also include detailed correspondence concerning the conduct which resulted in them being dismissed.

WO 138/75–7 contains the surviving records of Field Marshal Sir

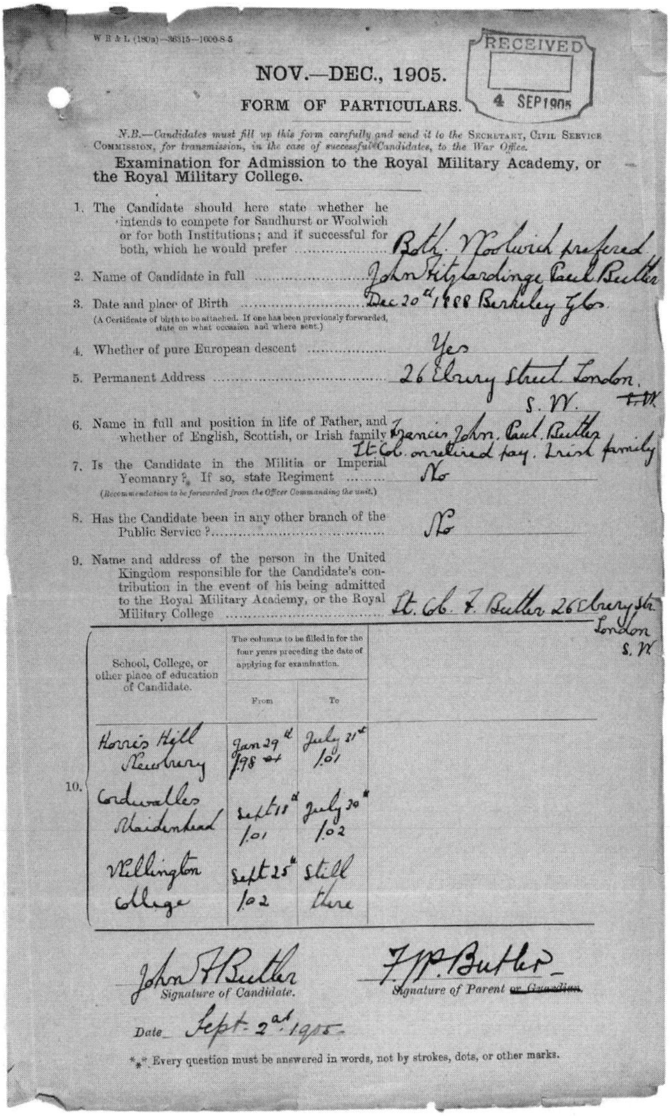

W R & L (180a)—36315—1000-8-5

RECEIVED 4 SEP 1905

NOV.—DEC., 1905.

FORM OF PARTICULARS.

N.B.—Candidates must fill up this form carefully and send it to the SECRETARY, CIVIL SERVICE COMMISSION, *for transmission, in the case of successful Candidates, to the War Office.*

Examination for Admission to the Royal Military Academy, or the Royal Military College.

1. The Candidate should here state whether he intends to compete for Sandhurst or Woolwich or for both Institutions; and if successful for both, which he would prefer .... Both. Woolwich prefered
2. Name of Candidate in full .... John Fitzhardinge Paul Butler
3. Date and place of Birth .... Dec 20th 1888 Berkeley Glos.
(A Certificate of birth to be attached. If one has been previously forwarded, state on what occasion and where sent.)
4. Whether of pure European descent .... Yes
5. Permanent Address .... 26 Ebury Street London. S.W.
6. Name in full and position in life of Father, and whether of English, Scottish, or Irish family Francis John Paul Butler Lt Col. on retired pay. Irish family
7. Is the Candidate in the Militia or Imperial Yeomanry? If so, state Regiment .... No
(Recommendation to be forwarded from the Officer Commanding the unit.)
8. Has the Candidate been in any other branch of the Public Service? .... No
9. Name and address of the person in the United Kingdom responsible for the Candidate's contribution in the event of his being admitted to the Royal Military Academy, or the Royal Military College .... Lt. Col. F. Butler 26 Ebury Str. London S.W.

10.

School, College, or other place of education of Candidate.	The columns to be filled in for the four years preceding the date of applying for examination. From	To
Horris Hill Newbury	Jan 29th 1898	July 21st 1901
Cordwalles Maidenhead	Sept 11th 1901	July 30th 1902
Wellington College	Sept 25th 1902	still there

John F Butler — *Signature of Candidate.*
F P Butler — *Signature of Parent* ~~or Guardian.~~

Date Sept. 2nd 1905

*** Every question must be answered in words, not by strokes, dots, or other marks.

Fig. 9 *Officer's Form of Particulars for entry into Sandhurst or Woolwich.* WO 339/6730

Douglas Haig. Whilst the amount of papers in these three files is impressive, they are primarily concerned with Haig's retired pay, his funeral in 1928 and the construction of a statue of him.

Other individuals whose files are in WO 138 include the poet Wilfred Owen and a number of significant generals of the war such as E.J.M. Stuart-Wortley, commander of 46 Division on 1 July 1916, and Brigadier General A.E. Aitken, commander of the forces that attempted to land at Tanga in German East Africa in 1914.

2.5.5 *The Royal Flying Corps and Royal Air Force (RFC and RAF)*

For a full explanation of the records of the RFC and RAF see *Air Force*

Records: A Guide for Family Historians by William Spencer, and also chapter 6.

In most cases officers of the RFC were commissioned into another unit before transferring into the RFC. Records of service of RFC officers can be found in WO 339 and WO 374 and can be traced using the methods described in 2.2, 2.2.1 and 2.3. In the Regt/Corps column of WO 338 (see 2.2), RFC may be found either alongside the original unit designation, or it may have replaced the original unit identity.

The other record series that contains RFC/RAF officers' records of service is AIR 76, which is available on microfilm. AIR 76 is arranged in alphabetical order by surname and contains the records of those officers who had left the RAF by early 1920. Interestingly, AIR 76 contains information about a number of officers of the RFC who were killed before the RAF was formed in April 1918.

2.5.6 *The Royal Naval Division (RND)*

The Royal Naval Division was formed in 1914 from some 30,000 surplus sailors for whom the Royal Navy had no ships. The RND saw service at Antwerp in 1914 and in Gallipoli in 1915, before returning to France in 1916.

Prior to 1916, the RND had been under Admiralty control and the division was manned by sailors and royal marines. In 1916, the RND was transferred to War Office control and was renamed the 63rd (RN) Division. With the transfer to War Office control the division finally acquired its own artillery and other supporting arms. Whilst most of the infantry were sailors and marines, the artillery and other support personnel were soldiers.

A collection of records of service of the Royal Naval Division can be found in ADM 339. This record series, which is available on microfiche, is split into three distinct parts: other ranks, officers and those members of the division who were discharged dead. All three sections are arranged in alphabetical order by surname.

As is usual with many records of service, the records in ADM 339 can provide basic biographical data, date of enlistment, information about leave, wounds, honours and awards, and also the name and address of the next of kin.

In most cases, records of service for officers of the RND can also be found in WO 339. When using the WO 338 index, RND will be found in the unit column. In many cases officers of the RND were Royal Naval Volunteer Reserve (RNVR) officers, and their records can be found in ADM 337. Research Guide Military Information Leaflet 71, 'The Royal Naval Volunteer Reserve, 1903–1919' provides data about the records in ADM 337.

The records in ADM 339 have been digitized and placed on DocumentsOnline, where it is possible to search for records by name of the individual.

2.5.7 WO 142

A card index of officers who served in the Royal Engineers Special (Gas) Brigade in the First World War can be found in WO 142/338 (surnames A–J) and 339 (surnames K–Y). These cards provide full name, date of appointment to the Special Brigade, postings and appointments, date of wounds or death (as appropriate) and date of demobilization.

2.6 The Army List

The *Army List* was, and still is, the official listing of all those officers holding a commission in the British Army. There was also an *Indian Army List*. The prime purpose of the *Army List* is to list the names of officers, giving the dates of their commissions and the unit they are serving in.

Copies of the *Army List* are available on the open shelves in the Open Reading Room and Library at Kew. Copies of the *Indian Army List* are available in the National Archives Library. Further copies of the *Indian Army List*, an almost complete run, are available on the open shelves in the Asia, Pacific and Africa Collections Reading Room at the British Library.

During the First World War period there were a number of different *Army Lists* whose contents varied according to when they were published. The most frequently published list was the monthly *Army List* which listed all officers whether they were Regular Army, Territorial Force (later Army) or reserve of army officers, giving their commission dates in the ranks they held at the time the list was published and the units they were serving in.

By using the monthly *Army Lists* it is possible to follow the promotions of an officer, and to see which unit(s) he served in.

The quarterly and half yearly *Army Lists* contain information only on officers holding permanent commissions. These lists are arranged by rank and then in graduation order, i.e. the date upon which an officer was promoted to a given rank. By using these lists it is possible to find information such as date of birth, date of first and subsequent commissions, staff appointments, courses the officer has attended and brief details concerning war service. The War Services section of these lists, published in January, provide information about the campaigns the officers were involved in and any medals they were awarded for those campaigns. The quarterly *Army Lists* were published in January, April, July and October.

There is a name index in the back of each *Army List* that refers you to a given column or page number within the List, with some officers having more than one entry in the index.

Army Lists can be used to see how the Army listed officers' surnames. This is especially important if the officer had a hyphenated surname, as the arrangement of the name may help you to find an officer in the medal index cards.

The monthly *Army Lists* include the units and officers of the Dominion forces that served as part of the British Army.

2.7   Other Printed Lists

There are a number of other printed lists concerning officers that are available at the National Archives. Some of these lists concern officers who died during the war and they are mentioned in the appropriate chapter. Many regimental histories, some of which are available in the National Archives Library, contain lists of officers. *A List of Commissioned Medical Officers of The Army 1660–1960* lists members of the Regular Army who were commissioned into the RAMC. A list of the Regular Army members of the Durham Light Infantry can be found in *Officers of the Durham Light Infantry Vol 1 (Regulars)* by Malcolm McGregor, available in the National Archives Library.

Senior officers and War Office civil servants, many of whom were former Army officers, can be found in the *War Office List*, copies of which can be found in the Open Reading Room.

2.8   Disability Pension Files (PIN 26)

A small number of disability pension files maintained by the Ministry of Pensions can be found in PIN 26/19924–54 and 21066–22756. Arranged in alphabetical order, these files contain brief information about the individuals' service and more about their medical histories and the payment of the pensions they were awarded. It is possible to search PIN 26 by name on the Catalogue.

2.9 The King's African Rifles and West African Frontier Force

Many officers of the British Army saw service in the King's African Rifles (KAR) or in the West African Frontier Force (WAFF) in either the Gold Coast Regiment, Nigeria Regiment or Sierra Leone Battalion. Such attachments are recorded in the *Army List*, where relevant sections for these African units can be found.

Correspondence of the KAR and WAFF can be found in CO 534/18–32 and CO 445/34–49 respectively.

2.10 Case Studies

Due to the sheer number of officers' files preserved in WO 138, WO 339 and WO 374 it is impossible to describe examples of them all. There are many records common to all officers and many, of course, which are unique. The stimulus for researching the career of an officer of the First World War can come from a number of different sources. What now follows are just two examples.

2.10.1 *Hedley John A'Bear*

Hedley John A'Bear was born at Waltham St Lawrence in Berkshire in 1893. Along with many young men he was a volunteer and he joined the Army on 2 September 1914 by enlisting into the Queen's Royal West Surrey Regiment at Guildford. Given the service number G2085, Private A'Bear was described as 5 feet 7¼ inches tall, with a fresh complexion, brown eyes and dark brown hair. With numerous other recruits Hedley joined the newly formed 7th Battalion, Queen's Royal West Surrey Regiment and along with the remainder of the unit went overseas on 27 July 1915. The battalion was part of the 55th Brigade, 18 (Eastern) Division.

Private A'Bear must have been a good soldier for he was promoted to the rank of corporal on 19 October 1915. Although not recorded in his record of service, he must have been granted a period of leave for on 1 January 1916 he married Winifred Mary Mason at Dunsfold in Surrey.

After he returned to France the 7th Battalion, Queen's Royal West Surrey Regiment were involved in the attack on Montauban on 1 July 1916, the first day of the battle of the Somme. The battalion suffered some 532 casualties and on 8 July Corporal A'Bear was promoted to sergeant. For his service on the Somme Sergeant A'Bear was awarded the Military Medal, which was announced in the *London Gazette* on 6 January 1917.

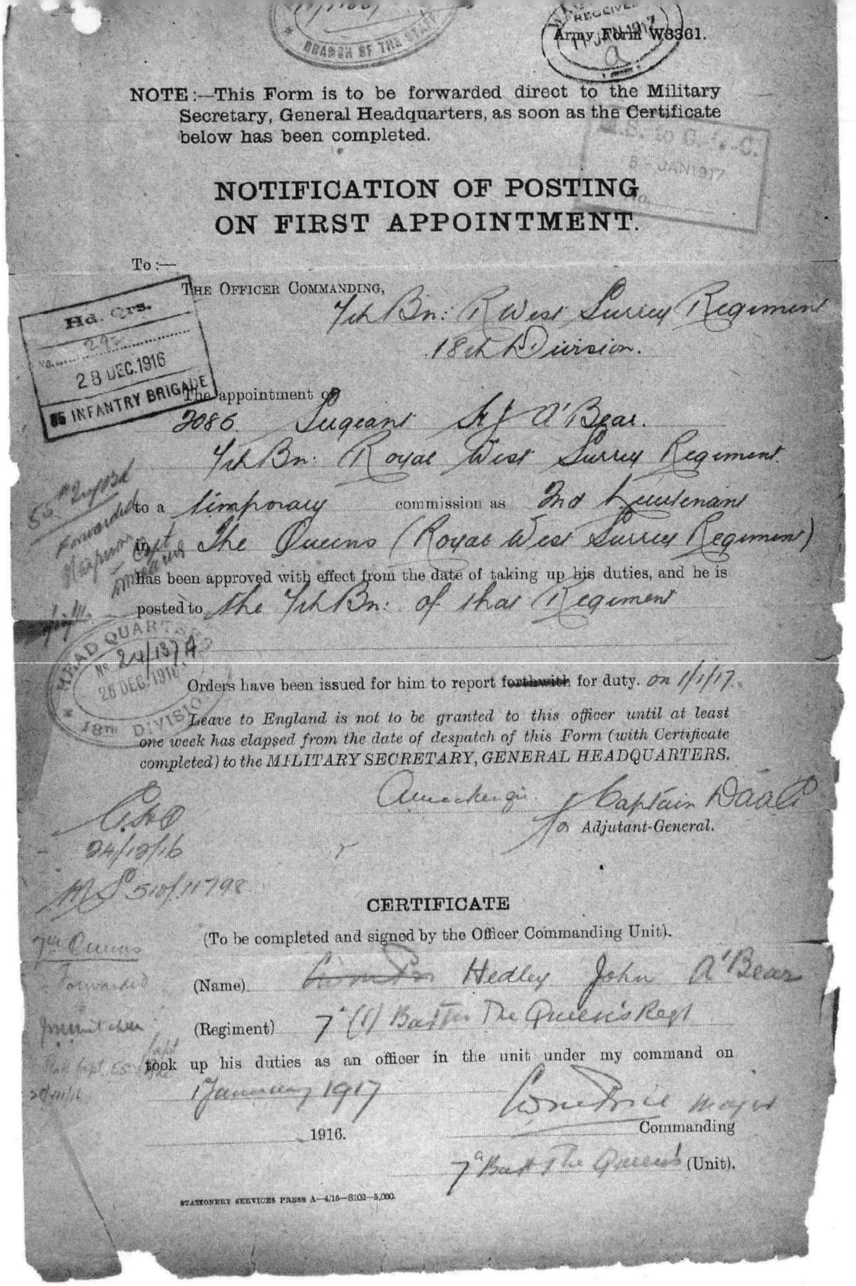

Army Form W3361.

NOTE:—This Form is to be forwarded direct to the Military Secretary, General Headquarters, as soon as the Certificate below has been completed.

NOTIFICATION OF POSTING ON FIRST APPOINTMENT.

To:—

THE OFFICER COMMANDING,

7th Bn: R West Surrey Regiment
18th Division.

The appointment of
3086 Sergeant H J A'Bear.
7th Bn: Royal West Surrey Regiment

to a temporary commission as 2nd Lieutenant
in The Queens (Royal West Surrey Regiment)
has been approved with effect from the date of taking up his duties, and he is posted to the 7th Bn: of that Regiment

Orders have been issued for him to report ~~forthwith~~ for duty. on 1/1/17.

Leave to England is not to be granted to this officer until at least one week has elapsed from the date of despatch of this Form (with Certificate completed) to the MILITARY SECRETARY, GENERAL HEADQUARTERS.

Captain
for Adjutant-General.

CERTIFICATE

(To be completed and signed by the Officer Commanding Unit).

(Name) Hedley John A'Bear

(Regiment) 7th (1) Batt The Queen's Regt

took up his duties as an officer in the unit under my command on 1 January 1917

1916.

Major
Commanding
7th Batt The Queens (Unit).

STATIONERY SERVICES PRESS A—4/16—S102—5,000.

Fig. 10 *Notification of first appointment for an officer in the field.* WO 339/117622

After 1915 nearly all officers granted commissions had to have seen service in the ranks.

According to A'Bear's record of service he was discharged to commission on 24 December 1916. Rather than return to England for further training A'Bear was trained in France, for it is noted in the unit war diary of the 7th Battalion, Queen's Royal West Surrey Regiment (WO 95/2051) on 1 January 1917 that 2nd Lieutenant H.J. A'Bear joined the battalion from GHQ Cadet School.

Second Lieutenant H.J. A'Bear first appears in the *Army List* in

March 1917 on page 916.

Official notification of 2nd Lieutenant H.J. A'Bear joining his battalion in the field is preserved in his record of service. What is interesting about his commission in the field is that he rejoined his old unit, rather than being posted to a new one as frequently happened.

Second Lieutenant A'Bear is next noted in the unit war diary as leading a patrol on 23 February. Further reference to A'Bear is made on 3 June 1917, when he is noted as moving from A Company to D Company and also taking command of the company with the rank of acting Captain.

In early July, the 18th Division were holding a section of the front near Zillebeke, east-south-east of Ypres. The 7th Battalion, Queen's Royal West Surrey Regiment, 55th Infantry Brigade, were holding the left flank of the Divisional position. According to the 18th Division General Headquarters diary (WO 95/2016) the division were dispersed in positions shown on 1:20000 Map 28NW/NE at 123a58.40.

The next, and unfortunately final, relevant entry in the unit war diary records that on 10 July 1917 Captain H.J. A'Bear and 2nd Lieutenant A.J.F. Osborne, both of A Company, were killed in company HQ, Lovers Walk, by shell. Captain A'Bear was one of only three officers of the battalion killed in July 1917.

Second Lieutenant/Acting Captain H.J. A'Bear MM is buried in Reninghelst New Military Cemetery, southwest of Ypres, in plot three, row F, grave eight.

The remaining contents of his record of service relate to the settling of his estate and the return of his personal effects to his next of kin, Mrs H.J. A'Bear, Rectory Cottage, Hascombe, Nr Godalming.

The sources used to create this case study include the medal index cards (WO 372), the *Army List*, the unit war diary of the 7th Battalion, Queen's Royal West Surrey Regiment (WO 95/2051), the Commonwealth War Graves Commission website (see 15.3.3) and H.J. A'Bear's record of service in WO 339/117622.

2.10.2 *Robert George Hopewell*

Robert George Hopewell was born in Nottingham in 1883. Enlisting as a private in the 10th Battalion, Notts and Derby Regiment on 24 September 1914, he was given the regimental number 10/17403. On his attestation, Hopewell gave his age as 31 years and 302 days and his occupation as contractor and bleaching machine manufacturer.

The 10th Notts and Derby Regiment was assigned to the 51st Infantry Brigade, 17th (Northern) Division and they arrived in France on 14 July 1915.

Obviously marked out as a potential officer, Private Hopewell only served in France with the 10th Notts and Derby Regiment until 5 August when he was discharged to a commission.

Full details about Robert Hopewell's service in France is not contained in his record of service, but the end of his career whilst serving with the 17th Service Battalion, Notts and Derby Regiment (Welbeck Rangers) is.

Appointed at some time after his commission to the 17th Battalion, Notts and Derby Regiment, Hopewell eventually rose to the rank of captain and it was whilst holding this rank that he was killed in action on the Somme on 3 September 1916. According to the unit war diary, Captain Hopewell was one of five officers killed on the same day. At the time of his death his battalion was serving in the 117th Infantry Brigade, part of the 39th Division.

On 3 September 1916, the 17th Notts and Derby Regiment took part in operations on the Ancre, specifically the attack on German trenches at Hamel. Starting the days with 20 officers and 650 other ranks, the battalion sustained over 450 casualties.

At the time of his death, Hopewell's widow Gladys was living at 39 Langtry Grove, New Basford, Nottingham. Although Gladys received her husband's estate, which was valued at £1847, 8 shillings and 11 pence, his personal military effects were sent to his brother Noah who lived in Old Basford.

Captain R.G. Hopewell's record of service, which contains his attestation papers and papers relating to his estate, can be found in WO 339/37823.

3 OTHER RANKS' RECORDS OF SERVICE

The files preserved in the record series WO 363, WO 364, WO 398, WO 400 and PIN 26 represent some 2.8 million individuals, most of whom saw operational service overseas. All of the files are unique, for while many shared a similar war experience, their careers could be so different.

The reasons why the records discussed in this chapter are the way that they are is mentioned in 1.1.

There is no such thing as a normal First World War record of service. Whilst many of the records contain Army Forms, which are common to most files, the files really do vary. Some files may be a single sheet, others may run to over 60 pages. There are a number of forms, which if they are found in the file of the person you are looking for, will alone be so informative that they will provide you with most of the data you seek. It is possible, however, that you will need to refer to a number of different forms found in a record, together with other records discussed in this book, in order to recreate something resembling a record of service.

This chapter cannot explain all of the different types of Army Forms that can be found in these records, but all those that are significant are covered below.

Originally a soldier's record would have consisted of an attestation sheet, of which there are over 10 different varieties depending upon date of enlistment, period of service and terms of engagement. Over seven different attestation forms can be found in either WO 363 or WO 364. The most common include the following:

AF B 141. Short Service 3 Years
AF B 2512. Short Service 3 Years. Duration of the War with the Colours and Reserve
AF E 501. Territorial Force 4 Years Service in the United Kingdom
AF B 2505. Short Service Duration of the War
AF B 2515. Enrolment Paper and Record of Service
AF B 311. Short Service 3 Years
AF B 111. Short Service 1 Years Service with the Colours 3 Years Reserve

An example of an attestation form can be seen in Fig. 14.

On all attestation papers or enrolment forms it is usual to find the information given by recruits when they went to enlist. In most cases the age and physical description of the soldier, his place of birth and any former service and occupation can be found. In some cases data concerning the next of kin may also be present. Kept within the attestation documents would usually be a conduct sheet and medical history sheet. If the soldier was a member of the Territorial Army, then an Imperial Service Obligation (AF E 624) form consenting to overseas service may be found. One of the most significant forms that might be found in a file is the Army Form B 103: Casualty Form-Active Service (see Fig. 13). On this form was recorded all of the most useful information about a soldier: his service details, his date of enlistment, promotions, awards, leave, transfers and anything else relating to him as an individual that the Army needed to know about. In short, the AF B 103 contains everything you might need to know about a soldier on one piece of paper. The AF B 103 was common to the whole Army, officer and other ranks, male and female.

At the end of a man's army career he would be discharged. This entailed the completion of another set of forms. Of these forms the most useful is the Personal Protection or Identity Certificate (PIC) (Army Form Z11), which provided information about age, physical description, his marital status and unit details. It also gave the man's address.

In many files it is possible to find a variety of other forms of correspondence, much of which relates to a soldier's employment before or after enlistment. This type of correspondence, whilst not containing much information concerning the war, can provide useful information about the man, his non-military life and his family.

Prior to the records of service being centralized at the War Office records repository, they were kept and administered by a number of regional records offices. Each of these regional records offices was responsible for looking after a number of regiments or corps, and it was also the responsibility of these records offices to send out letters to the next of kin of soldiers who had died.

Using the records in WO 363 and WO 364 is like a voyage of discovery. You know what you want to find and know where to look, but what you find can be either disappointing or revelatory.

(2)
WIDOWS' FORM 25.

Case No. 23

Regiment 28th London T.F

Number, Rank and Name of Soldier 764970 Pte. John Allum

Date, place and cause of death 30-10-17 B.E.F France Killed in Action.

Date of Marriage 1-3-10 (m/c. recd)

Name and address of widow Mrs Eleanor Victoria Allum (Born 24-2-83)
28 Dacre Hill
Rock Ferry
Cheshire

Names and dates of birth of children   Born   Pension Expires

Award Proposed—   a week

Class V

13/9 Widow

for Pension

With effect from the 27.5.18.

M.E.S.
Separation Allowance
paid to   26.5.18.

Approved under Article 11, Royal Warrant of the 29th March, 1917. or 3.5.18.

Return 1   Certificate to Widow (Widows' Form 5)

OCl   (sent 31.1.18 OCl)

(681) Wt. 2070/135 30x. 4/17 C.P., Ltd. G 15.95²
(1119) Wt. 18607/345 30x. 7/17

3.1 The 'Burnt Records' (WO 363)

The records in this series are the records that survived the fire at Arnside Street on 8 September 1940. Not only are they fire damaged, but they are also water damaged. Consequently the originals are so fragile the only way they can be made available is on microfilm. How these records were arranged before the fire is unknown, but they were put into an alphabetical sequence after the war.

The records in this series are for men who completed their service at any time between 1914 and 1920. Amongst the records can be found those of men who survived the war, men who died of wounds or disease and men who were killed in action. Also in WO 363 there are a number of files of men who were executed, including Joseph Stones and William Nelson. Many of the files concern men who were discharged as a result of sickness or wounds contracted or received during the war.

3.1.1 Arrangement

The original records in WO 363 are kept in 33,000 boxes. As the collection is so big, the only way it could be filmed was by letter of the alphabet. As there are a number of cameras doing the filming, the filming of the range of surnames of any given letter is not just started at the first name and then done in sequence — each camera has been given a specific range of surnames within a letter. As this is the case it is very important to consult the WO 363 catalogue for the letter of the alphabet you want and then find the relevant surname and forename(s). The first reel of WO 363 S (WO 363/S1), for example, may not cover a surname beginning with Sa but may start at Sl. All of the catalogues in WO 363 are arranged in alphabetical order by surname and not in piece number order.

The following statistics indicate the enormous size of this particular record collection and its associated problems:

NUMBER OF REELS OF MICROFILM PER LETTER

Letter	Reels	Letter	Reels	Letter	Reels	Letter	Reels
A	738	B	2679	C	1955	D	1143
E	609	F	1025	G	1496	H	2790
I	128	J	912	K	588	L	1088
M	2449	N	398	O	299	P	1717
Q	36	R	1750	S	3327	T	1405
U	45	V	117	W	2451	Y	138
Z	5						

Included in the figure for surnames beginning with the letter S are 562 reels of Smith, including 52 reels of John Smith!

3.2 The 'Unburnt Records' (WO 364)

The records in WO 364 are those records that the War Office recovered from other government departments at the end of the Second World War. The majority of these records came from the Ministry of Pensions and they primarily concern men who were discharged from the Army on account of sickness or wounds suffered between 1914 and 1920. A large number of files concern soldiers who had been discharged to pension before the war and who, by virtue of further service between 1914 and 1920, needed to have their pension payments altered on account of additional service.

WO 364 also contains a number of very interesting anomalies. Records of a number of soldiers who were discharged many years before the First World War, as far back as 1875, have been found in WO 364. A number of files of British men who served in the South African Infantry or Australian Imperial Force but who were discharged in Britain have also been found in this record series.

Most of the files in WO 364 contain not only the usual military-type records relating to enlistment, conduct and overseas service, but also detailed medical records relating to the disability for which the individual was granted a pension. Many of these medical records contain descriptions of wounds and the date and place the soldiers were when they were wounded. This information can be used when looking at the unit war diaries in WO 95.

3.2.1 *Arrangement*
Unlike WO 363, which is arranged by letter of the alphabet and then by name, WO 364 is arranged in alphabetical order. There are, however, four A–Z sequences in WO 364:

WO 364/1–4912	A–Z
WO 364/4913–15	A–Z
WO 364/5000–5802	A–Z
WO 364/5803–4	A–W (miss-sorts)

3.3 Women's Army Auxiliary Corps (WO 398)

Conceived in early 1917, and formally established by Army Council

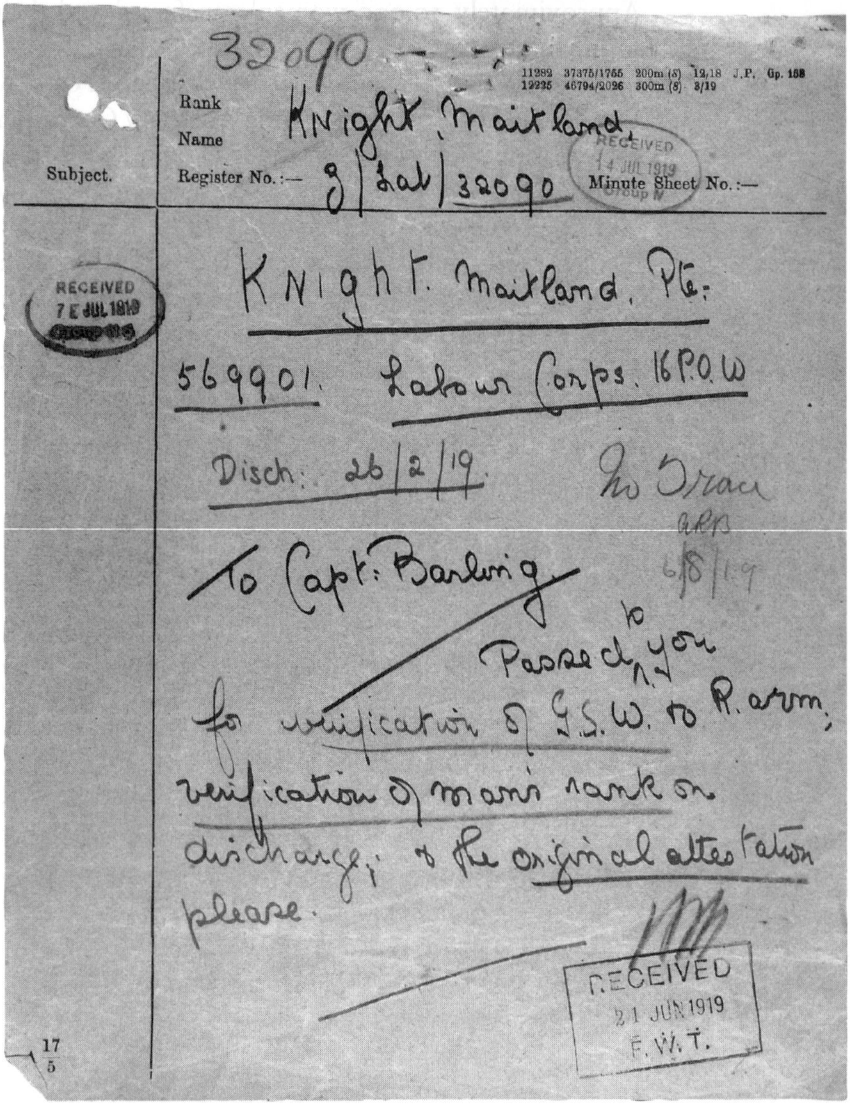

32090

11282 37375/1765 200m (S) 12/18 J.P. Gp. 158
12295 46794/2026 300m (S) 3/19

Subject.

Rank
Name Knight, Maitland.
Register No.:— G/Lab/32090

RECEIVED 14 JUL 1919 Group N

Minute Sheet No.:—

RECEIVED 7 E JUL 1919

KNIGHT. Maitland. Pte.

569901. Labour Corps. 16 P.O.W

Disch: 26/2/19. No trace

ARB 6/8/19

To Capt. Barling

Passed to you for verification of G.S.W. to R. arm; verification of man's rank on discharge; & the original attestation please.

RECEIVED 21 JUN 1919 F.W.T.

17
5

Fig. 12 *Minute sheet from within a Ministry of Pensions file for a soldier discharged on account of sickness of wounds.* PIN 26/8568

Instruction No. 1068 of July 1917, the Women's Army Auxiliary Corps (WAAC) was established upon the recommendations of Lieutenant General H.M. Lawson, who suggested that women be employed in France.

Organized into four sections: Cookery, Mechanical, Clerical and Miscellaneous, the women in the corps were split into 'Officials' (the officers) and 'Members' (the other ranks). Renamed the Queen Mary's Army Auxiliary Corps (QMAAC) in April 1918, the corps would eventually employ some 57,000 women at home and overseas. Those women who served at Royal Flying Corps airfields transferred to the Women's Royal Air Force when it was created in April 1918.

Approximately 10,000 women transferred and their records can be found in AIR 80.

Most files in WO 398 contain an Army Form W 3578 Form of Enrolment in the Women's Army Auxiliary Corps. This form provides information such as the age of the woman, her address, marital status and whether she was willing to serve overseas. If the member of the WAAC served overseas then an Army Form B 103 may be found.

One of the most informative forms that occur in WO 398 is the NSVW 3 National Service Department (Women's Section) Qualifications of Applicant form. This form tells you where the woman was born, her current address, any qualifications and work experience, and current occupation, together with the names of two referees.

As with all other service personnel, women also had an identification certificate, an Army Form W 3577, which gave a physical description and the home address of the holder.

The records in WO 398 comprise the surviving records of service of female other ranks of the Women's Auxiliary Army Corps (Queen Mary's Auxiliary Army Corps). There are no surviving records of service of female officers of the corps.

WO 398 has been digitized and placed on DocumentsOnline where it is possible to search by the name of the member of the QMAAC. There are 7,006 individuals in WO 398.

3.4 Digital Access to WO 363, WO 364 and WO 398

The records of service preserved in the National Archives in the series WO 363, WO 364 and WO 398 have — or are still being (WO 363) — digitized and are accessible via two different portals. Access to these records requires further elucidation.

3.4.1 WO 363 and WO 364

The two series of other ranks papers in WO 363 and WO 364 are accessible via the Ancestry website at *www.ancestry.co.uk*. There are a number of benefits from digitization, but there are number of pitfalls which the user needs to know about.

Access to the microfilms of WO 363 and WO 364 requires an understanding of how each series is arranged and how to apply the name of the soldier you seek to WO 363 and WO 364 catalogues. By digitizing the records in WO 363 and WO 364, the records of separate individuals have been itemized for the first time.

Advice is required on the descriptions of WO 363 and WO 364 on the ancestry website. WO 363 is described as service records and this is a satisfactory description. WO 364, however, is described as 'pension records', which is confusing as they are most certainly not. The National Archives description of WO 364 is 'service records derived from pension claims'. To understand the origins and content of WO 364 see 3.2 above.

The searching of WO 363 and WO 364 on *www.ancestry.co.uk* is slightly different. For WO 363 you can search by forename(s) or initial(s), surname, estimated date and place of birth, regiment(s)/ corps, regimental/corps number(s) and by keyword. For WO 364 this is almost the same, but currently you are unable to search by regiment(s)/corps. This anomaly will be rectified on completion of the digitization of WO 363.

At the time of writing only WO 364 has been digitized in its entirety. The project to digitize the whole of WO 363 is due for completion in 2009.

If you find papers on *www.ancestry.co.uk* it helps to understand how the records are produced in order to ensure that you get all of the pages of any given individual.

When the records in WO 363 and WO 364 were being digitized, a computer algorithm was created to search for certain types of army forms, usually either the attestation (joining) or discharge (leaving) form. When a search finds something relevant to the search term(s) you used, it will tell you how many pages there are in the record. When you click to view the pages, the first page you see (the landing page) will almost certainly be either an attestation or discharge form. The landing page in a man's record of service is frequently not always the first page in the sequence of pages. The reason for this is because the papers were used by the War Office and MOD over many years, and whilst the collection of papers for a man were usually kept together, their proper order may now be out of sequence after many years' use.

The actual position of a landing page in a man's record of service is not indicated (whether it is page 1, 7, 25 or the last one). In order to see all of the pages of a given record, it may be necessary to use the back and forward arrows, looking carefully at every page, in order to see all that survives.

3.4.2 WO 398

The records of service of the Queen Mary's Army Auxiliary Corps in the series WO 398 have been digitized and placed on DocumentsOnline on the National Archives website (*www.nationalarchives.gov.uk*). It is possible to search WO 398 on DocumentsOnline by name and download and read any results. As with the records in WO 363, many of the surviving records are fire and water damaged and consequently may be difficult to read.

3.5 Household Cavalry Records (WO 400)

The records of service of men discharged from regiments of the Household Cavalry can be found in the series WO 400. The records in this series represent men from the Life Guards, Royal Horse Guards and the Household Battalion (which was only created during the First World War).

The records in WO 400 are arranged by regiment, in chronological ranges covering the date of discharge, and each group is arranged in alphabetical order. For the First World War period the following parts of WO 400 may be of interest.

Regiment	Discharge Dates	WO 400 Pieces
1st Life Guards	1859–1920	5–55
2nd Life Guards	1856–1919	87–166
Royal Horse Guards	1886–1919	230–85
Household Battalion	1916–1919	286–301

The records in the Household Battalion section of WO 400 cover mostly men who were killed in action or who were invalided out of the army.

These records are produced as original records and will need to be ordered on the document ordering system.

3.6 The Ministry of Pensions Records (PIN 26)

In PIN 26 are preserved 22,801 files of officers and other ranks, male and female, Army and Royal Navy, who were discharged from the services as a result of sickness or wounds contracted or received during the war. This record series also includes a number of files of dependants rather than the service personnel themselves. PIN 26 is only a two per cent sample of all of the files concerning service personnel who had pensions that were granted or administered by the Ministry of Pensions. However, a significant percentage of the remaining 98 per cent from which this sample was taken, can actually be found in WO 364.

The records in PIN 26 are arranged in a number of series within the collection. In most cases they are arranged in alphabetical order, and the catalogue often provides basic data about the reason for discharge.

One point to note about PIN 26 is the date range given for each file. As the files concern disability pensions paid to individuals, the dates given reflect the date an individual joined the armed forces and the date the pension or correspondence within the file ceased.

Amongst the files in PIN 26 are the records concerning a soldier who won the Victoria Cross at the defence of Rorke's Drift in January 1879, during the Zulu War, and a file for a soldier who was eventually hanged as a murderer. Both individuals saw service between 1914 and 1918.

The actual paper content of the files in PIN 26 is very similar to the records in WO 364: basic record of service, medical reports and assessments and pension calculations and awards. As in many cases the pensions ceased upon death of the individual, the files often contain death certificates.

The content of PIN 26 is arranged in the following sections, all of which are arranged in alphabetical order:

PIN 26/1–16683	Other ranks
PIN 26/19854–19923	Other ranks
PIN 26/19955–19984	Alternative disabled pensions
PIN 26/20287–21065	Pensioners living overseas
PIN 26/22757–22800	Other ranks

Forms
B. 2512
1

ORIGINAL

SHORT SERVICE.

(For the Duration of the War, with the Colours and in the Army Reserve).

FIT FOR GENERAL SERVICE

Card No.
849
I

1834

ATTESTATION OF

No. ~~1674~~   Name _John Parker_   Corps ~~Scottish Rifles~~   Household Bn

Questions to be put to the Recruit before Enlistment.

1. What is your Name?	1.	John Parker
2. What is your full Address?	2.	4 Purdie Street Burnbank, Hamilton
3. Are you a British Subject?	3.	Yes
4. What is your Age?	4.	18 Years 11 Months
5. What is your Trade or Calling?	5.	House Painter
6. Are you Married?	6.	No
7. Have you ever served in any branch of His Majesty's Forces, naval or military, if so*, which?	7.	No
8. Are you willing to be vaccinated or re-vaccinated?	8.	Yes
9. Are you willing to be enlisted for General Service?	9.	Yes
10. Did you receive a Notice, and do you understand its meaning, and who gave it to you?	10.	Yes Name .... Corps ....

11. Are you willing to serve upon the following conditions provided His Majesty should so long require your services?

For the duration of the War, at the end of which you will be discharged with all convenient speed. You will be required to serve for one day with the Colours and the remainder of the period in the Army Reserve, in accordance with the provisions of the Royal Warrant dated 20th Oct., 1915, until such time as you may be called up by order of the Army Council. If employed with Hospitals, depots of Mounted Units, or as a Clerk, etc., you may be retained after the termination of hostilities until your services can be spared, but such retention shall in no case exceed six months.

11.   Yes

3.3 Asso't Hamilton

I, _John Parker_ do solemnly declare that the above answers made by me to the above questions are true, and that I am willing to fulfil the engagements made.

John Parker SIGNATURE OF RECRUIT.

F. G. Bridges Signature of Witness.

OATH TO BE TAKEN BY RECRUIT ON ATTESTATION.

I, _John Parker_ swear by Almighty God, that I will be faithful and bear true Allegiance to His Majesty King George the Fifth, His Heirs, and Successors, and that I will, as in duty bound, honestly and faithfully defend His Majesty, His Heirs, and Successors, in Person, Crown, and Dignity against all enemies, and will observe and obey all orders of His Majesty, His Heirs and Successors, and of the Generals and Officers set over me. So help me God.

CERTIFICATE OF MAGISTRATE OR ATTESTING OFFICER.

The Recruit above named was cautioned by me that if he made any false answer to any of the above questions he would be liable to be punished as provided in the Army Act.

The above questions were then read to the Recruit in my presence.

I have taken care that he understands each question, and that his answer to each question has been duly entered as replied to, and the said Recruit has made and signed the declaration and taken the oath before me at _Hamilton_

on this 1st day of _Jun_ 1916.

Signature of the Justice _A. Thom Lt. Major_
Recruiting Officer.

26th Rec. Area.

† Certificate of Approving Officer.

I certify that this Attestation of the above-named Recruit is correct, and properly filled up, and that the required forms appear to have been complied with. I accordingly approve, and appoint him to the ‡ _Scottish Rifles_

If enlisted by special authority, Army Form B. 203 (or other authority for the enlistment) will be attached to the original attestation.

Date _27 6_ 1916.

Place _Hamilton_

Cocaine Lieut Col
_26th RA_   Approving Officer.

† The signature of the Approving Officer is to be affixed in the presence of the Recruit.
‡ Here insert the "Corps" for which the Recruit has been enlisted.

* If so, the Recruit is to be asked the particulars of his former service, and to produce, if possible, his Certificate of Discharge and Certificate of Character, which should be returned to him conspicuously endorsed in red ink, as follows, viz.—(Name) .... re-enlisted in the (Regiment) .... on the (Date) ....

As with nearly all the records at the National Archives, it is possible to search PIN 26 by name on the Catalogue. The surname of a subject individual is always listed, but in some cases only the initial rather than the full first name is given. In many cases the reason for discharge is given as either a code or an abbreviation. A full list of the codes and abbreviations can be found in the PIN 26 paper catalogue. Among the abbreviations, GSW is frequently seen and it is perhaps obvious to most what it stands for: Gun Shot Wound.

3.7 Files of Dead Chelsea Pensioners (WO 324)

WO 324 is a collection of some 269 files of soldiers who were at one time inmates at the Royal Hospital Chelsea. Arranged in alphabetical order, the files are more concerned with the soldiers' time in the hospital than with their military careers, although brief information about their service is usually included. The dates of the files reflect the dates when they entered the hospital and the dates when they died, not their service dates. It is possible to search WO 324 by name on the Catalogue.

3.8 The King's African Rifles and West African Frontier Force

During the First World War a large number of British Army NCOs served as instructors in either the King's African Rifles (KAR) or the West African Frontier Force (WAFF) (either the Gold Coast Regiment, the Nigeria Regiment or Sierra Leone Battalion). A number of these men were serving at the outbreak of the war; many volunteered after the war had started.

The correspondence of the West African Frontier Force, which includes plenty of information about operations of the WAFF and the soldiers serving in it, can be found in CO 445. The correspondence of the King's African Rifles can be found in CO 534.

A list of British Army NCOs serving in the KAR in September 1918, giving name, rank, number, parent regiment, battalion of the KAR and when they joined the KAR, can be found in CO 534/26 ff373–422.

3.9   The British West Indies Regiment

Although men of the British West Indies Regiment (BWIR) can be found in the medal records (see chapter 9), none of their records of service have been found in either WO 363 or WO 364. Some information about men of the BWIR can be found in CO 318 Colonial Office West Indies: General Correspondence. Examples of these records include a number of nominal rolls for 1915–16, which can be found in CO 318/336 and include a roll of the Bermuda Volunteer Rifle Corps, lists of wives eligible for separation pay and details of next of kin.

The cataloguing of CO 318 has been greatly improved over the last few years and it is now possible to search the series by name or subject on the Catalogue.

3.10   The Macedonian Mule Corps

Raised primarily in Cyprus and southern Greece for service as part of the logistical support for the British Army in a number of different operational theatres, an incomplete nominal roll and history of the corps can be found in WO 405/1.

3.11 Case Studies

The following case studies illustrate what can be found out about a member of the Women's Army Auxiliary Corps and ordinary British soldiers in the British Army.

3.11.1 *Agnes May Wordsall*

Agnes May Wordsall was born in Leicester on 28 August 1892. Little is known about her prior to when she enlisted in the WAAC, but she had been working as a clerk and typist for 10 years before her enlistment on 6 March 1917. On enlistment, Wordsall was living with her mother at 9 Western Road, Derby and was described as 5 feet 3½ inches tall, of medium build, with mid-brown hair and grey/blue eyes. She was 24 years old and was single.

Given the WAAC number 681, Wordsall volunteered for service overseas and in June 1917 she sailed for France from Folkestone. By going to France Wordsall qualified for a British War and Victory Medal.

Little is known of her service in France. However, from her AF B 103, she is recorded as being in hospital at Etaples in February 1918. Granted leave to the UK in August 1918, Wordsall returned to France and served there until at least October 1919. Agnes May Wordsall served in the Army until 20 November 1919, when her engagement came to an end.

Whilst information on her time in the Army is scarce, she must have been very good at her job, for on 3 June 1919 she was awarded the Medal of the Order of the British Empire, which went on to be announced in the *London Gazette* on 28 January 1920.

Agnes May Wordsall's papers can be found in WO 398/237.

3.11.2 *William Henry Spencer*

The following individual is not related to the author, but just provides a typical example of a soldier's career that can be found in WO 363 or WO 364.

William Henry Spencer was born at Nechells in Birmingham in 1892. He joined the Army in the rush of volunteers on 28 September 1914. Although on his attestation form his occupation was given as Electroplater and Silver Finisher, W.H. Spencer opted to join the Royal Army Medical Corps and was given the service number 38280. At the time of his attestation Spencer was described as 5 feet 6 inches tall with a fresh complexion, blue eyes and black hair.

Unlike many of the men who joined the Army in the first months of the war, Private Spencer was not single, having married Louise Greenway at Nechells on 16 December 1911. He was also a father, his son Howard William Spencer having been born at Aston in Birmingham on 25 October 1913.

According to the Army Form B 103 Casualty Form — Active Service, Private Spencer joined 55 Field Ambulance and sailed for France on 26 July 1915. This unit was part of 18 Division. Private Spencer saw service with this unit until 1918 when he transferred to 42 Field Ambulance.

Other information contained in Private Spencer's records includes the fact that he was punished on two occasions, once for being drunk and once for insubordination and not complying with an order. For these offences he was given 14 days confined to barracks and the loss of the one good conduct badge that he had been awarded on 28 September 1916.

The AF B 103 notes a number of periods of leave and also records that he was admitted as a patient to 55 Field Ambulance suffering from gonorrhoea on 16 September 1918.

Private Spencer served in the Army for 4 years 179 days, including the period 25 July 1915–13 March 1919 overseas. Awarded the 1914/15 Star, British War Medal and Victory Medal, he was finally discharged on 12 April 1919.

Private Spencer's record of service can be found in WO 363/S 1520.

3.11.3 *John Allum*

John Allum appears from his record of service to have been a conscript, for he did not joined the Army until 15 January 1917. At the time of his attestation he was 35 years old and employed as a hospital steward. As a hospital steward you might have expected John Allum to join the Royal Army Medical Corps but he actually joined the 2/28th Battalion, the London Regiment, known as the Artists Rifles.

After his training, 764970 Private John Allum embarked at Southampton on 14 May 1917 and arrived at Le Havre the following day. Transferred to the 1/28th London Regiment on 19 May 1917, little is known about Allum's experience on the Western Front.

On 24 June 1917, Allum was sent to 24 Field Ambulance suffering from influenza. He rejoined his battalion on 11 July, in time to take part in operations around Ypres.

The 1/28th London Regiment was one of the infantry battalions in the 190th Infantry Brigade, which was part of the 63rd (Royal Naval) Division.

The 63rd (RN) Division was heavily involved in the third Battle of Ypres (Passchendaele). On 30 October 1917, the 190th Infantry Brigade made a second attack on the German defences near Poelcappelle sustaining many casualties for little gain. It was during this day's action that John Allum was killed.

John Allum left behind a widow, Eleanor, who at the time of his death was living in Rock Ferry in Cheshire.

Awarded a pension of 13 shillings and nine pence a week, John Allum's widow moved to Edmonton in Canada in 1919. The Ministry of Pensions widow's form for Eleanor Allum can be seen in PIN 82/2. (see Fig. 11)

John Allum has no known grave and is commemorated on panel 153 of the Tyne Cot Memorial.

4 NURSES

Although numerous nurses from a variety of different organizations saw service during the First World War, only the records of those nurses who were military nurses are discussed here. The records of nurses of the Voluntary Aid Detachments (VADs) are held by the Red Cross Archives (see 15.3.6).

At the outbreak of the First World War there were two army nursing services: the Queen Alexandra's Imperial Military Nursing Service (QAIMNS) and the Territorial Force Nursing Service (TFNS). The QAIMNS was also split into two parts, the regulars and the reserve, the QAIMNS(R). The QAIMNS was established by Royal Warrant on 27 March 1902 from the Army Nursing Service (ANS), while the TFNS was formed in 1908 to support the Territorial Army, which had been created under the Territorial Reserve Forces Act of 1907.

Although nurses served in most operational theatres, only a list of those arriving in France is known (WO 95/3982). To discover if a nurse served overseas it is necessary to locate either a record of service or a campaign medal index card.

4.1 Records of Service

The records of service of military nurses can be found in the record series WO 399. They are arranged in two sections: QAIMNS with the QAIMNS(R), and the TFNS. Both sections are then arranged alphabetically.

Although the series list for WO 399 describes the dates of the records as covering 1914–22, they actually cover the careers of those nurses whose service was completed prior to 1939. As long as the nurse saw no service either during or later than the Second World War, then the record may be in WO 399.

WO 339 contains the records of 15,792 nurses. The records of the QAIMNS and QAIMNS(R) are in WO 399/1–9349 and the records of

Fig. 16 *A nurse's offer to serve in His Majesty's Forces.*
WO 399/6979

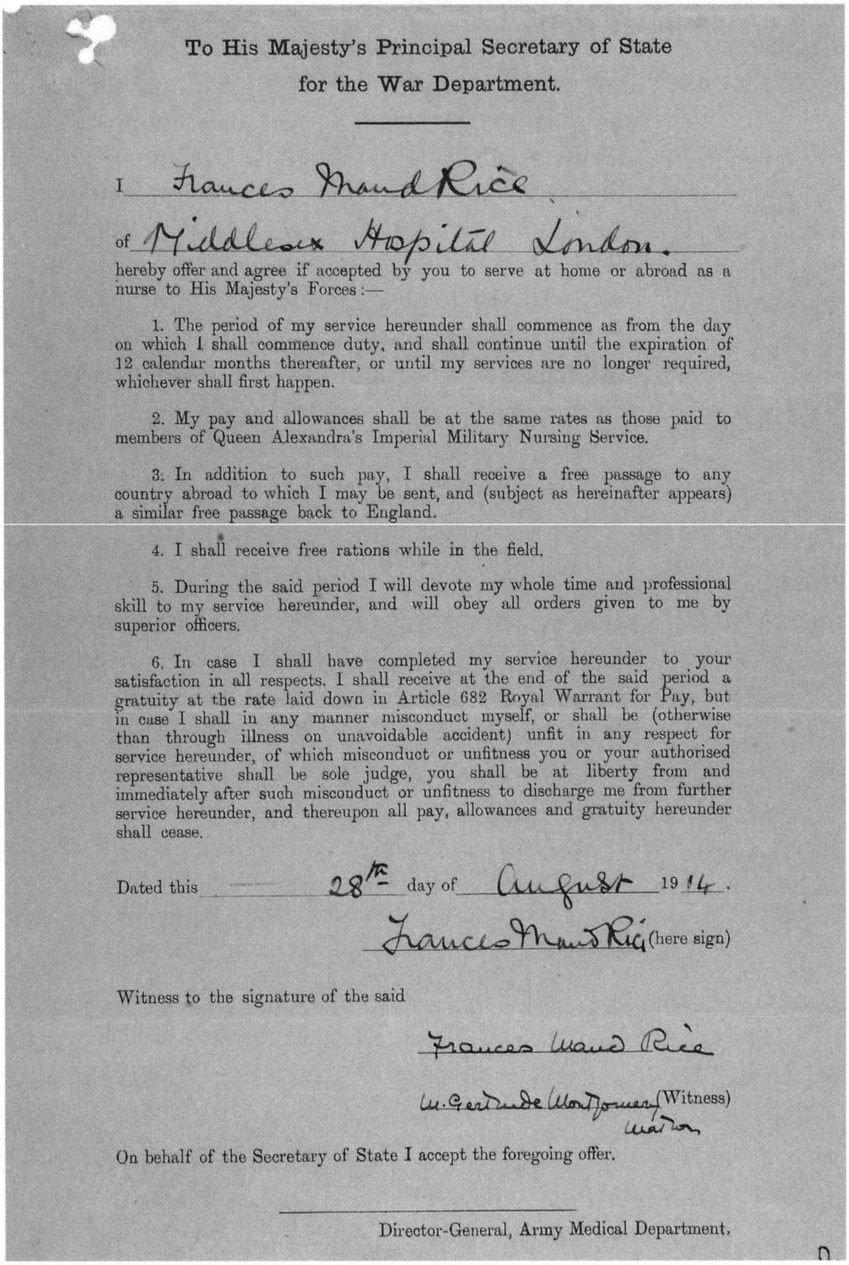

To His Majesty's Principal Secretary of State
for the War Department.

I *Frances Maud Rice*

of *Middlesex Hospital London.*

hereby offer and agree if accepted by you to serve at home or abroad as a nurse to His Majesty's Forces :—

1. The period of my service hereunder shall commence as from the day on which I shall commence duty, and shall continue until the expiration of 12 calendar months thereafter, or until my services are no longer required, whichever shall first happen.

2. My pay and allowances shall be at the same rates as those paid to members of Queen Alexandra's Imperial Military Nursing Service.

3. In addition to such pay, I shall receive a free passage to any country abroad to which I may be sent, and (subject as hereinafter appears) a similar free passage back to England.

4. I shall receive free rations while in the field.

5. During the said period I will devote my whole time and professional skill to my service hereunder, and will obey all orders given to me by superior officers.

6. In case I shall have completed my service hereunder to your satisfaction in all respects. I shall receive at the end of the said period a gratuity at the rate laid down in Article 682 Royal Warrant for Pay, but in case I shall in any manner misconduct myself, or shall be (otherwise than through illness on unavoidable accident) unfit in any respect for service hereunder, of which misconduct or unfitness you or your authorised representative shall be sole judge, you shall be at liberty from and immediately after such misconduct or unfitness to discharge me from further service hereunder, and thereupon all pay, allowances and gratuity hereunder shall cease.

Dated this _____ 28th day of August 19 14.

Frances Maud Rice (here sign)

Witness to the signature of the said

Frances Maud Rice

M. Gertrude Montgomery (Witness)
Matron

On behalf of the Secretary of State I accept the foregoing offer.

_____
Director-General, Army Medical Department.

the TFNS are in WO 399/9350–15792. Although the records are arranged in alphabetical order, for those nurses who married during their service, it is possible to find files listed under the later married name rather than the maiden name under which many of them started their service.

It is possible to search for records of service in WO 339 by the name of the subject individual on the Catalogue.

4.2 Medals

Any nurse who served in an operational theatre was eligible for the same campaign medal as her male counterparts. See chapter 9 for details about campaign medals. Although nurses had officer status, they were not eligible for officers' gallantry awards. Nurses were eligible for the Military Medal (MM) and the Royal Red Cross (RRC). Nurses were also eligible for awards under the Most Excellent Order of the British Empire. For information about the MM and RRC and other awards for gallantry and meritorious service, see chapter 10.

4.3 Disability Pensions (PIN 26)

A small number of disability pensions files kept by the Ministry of Pensions about nurses who were given pensions on account of wounds or sickness received or contracted during the war can be found in PIN 26/19985–20286. These files are in alphabetical order and can be searched by name on the Catalogue.

4.4 *The Nursing Times*

The newspaper of the nursing profession during the First World War was *The Nursing Times*. The newspaper is still in print.

Information about military nurses, appointments and awards were published in *The Nursing Times* during the war and access to digitized copies of the paper is available via the archives at *www.rcn.org.uk*. It is possible to search the paper by subject or name.

4.5 Case Studies

4.5.1 *Frances Maud Rice*

Frances Maud Rice was born in 1874, the daughter of Colonel Cecil Rice, formerly of the 72nd Foot (Seaforth Highlanders), who had seen active service in the Crimea 1854–6 and the Indian Mutiny 1857–8. At the time when she became a military nurse her father was living at Kingscott House, East Grinstead in Sussex.

Although there is no information stating when she qualified as a nurse, the earliest indication that Sister Rice was already a nurse at the outbreak of the First World War is a letter dated 26 August 1914

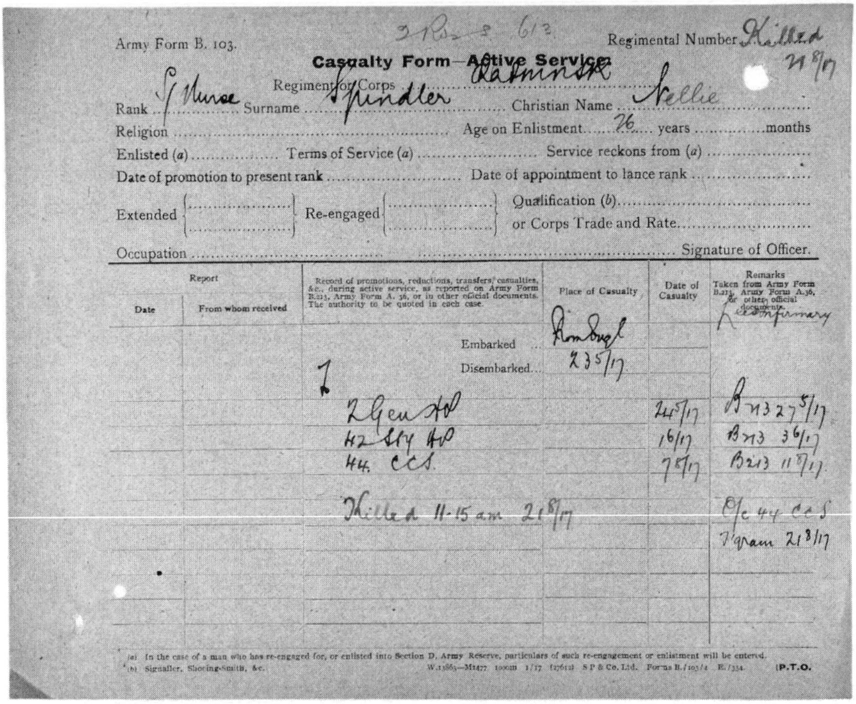
Army Form B. 103. Regimental Number Killed 21/8/17

Casualty Form—Active Service

Regiment or Corps

Rank S/Nurse Surname Spindler Christian Name Nellie

Religion ... Age on Enlistment 26 years ... months

Enlisted (a) ... Terms of Service (a) ... Service reckons from (a) ...

Date of promotion to present rank ... Date of appointment to lance rank ...

Extended ... Re-engaged ... Qualification (b) ... or Corps Trade and Rate ...

Occupation ... Signature of Officer.

Report: Date	Report: From whom received	Record of promotions, reductions, transfers, casualties, &c., during active service, as reported on Army Form B.213, Army Form A. 36, or in other official documents. The authority to be quoted in each case.	Place of Casualty	Date of Casualty	Remarks Taken from Army Form B.213, Army Form A.36, or other official documents.
		Embarked			
		Disembarked	23/5/17		
		2 Gen Hos		24/5/17	B213 27/5/17
		42 Sty Hos		1/6/17	B213 3/6/17
		44 CCS		7/8/17	B213 11/8/17
		Killed 11.15 am 21/8/17			O/c 44 CCS Tgram 21/8/17

(a) In the case of a man who has re-engaged for, or enlisted into Section D, Army Reserve, particulars of such re-engagement or enlistment will be entered.
(b) Signaller, Shoeing-Smith, &c.

(P.T.O.)

Fig. 17 *The Army Form B 103 of Staff Nurse Nellie Spindler, recording her exact time of death in August 1917.* WO 399/7850

from a Captain in the RAMC (T) at the 4 General Hospital, certifying that she was fit for foreign service. Two days later Sister Rice officially offered her services to the Secretary of State for War (Fig. 16). The acceptance of this offer led to Sister Rice joining the Territorial Force Nursing Service (TFNS).

Sister Rice embarked for France on 24 September 1914 and arrived there on the 26th, where she joined 5 General Hospital. By entering France before 22 November 1914, Sister Rice qualified for the 1914 Star.

During the next two years Sister Rice was to see extensive service at a number of different medical units on the Western Front. After service at 5 General Hospital she went to 2 Ambulance Train, 20 General Hospital, 24 General Hospital and 29 Casualty Clearing Station. On 28 September 1916, whilst at 29 Casualty Clearing Station, Sister Rice was invalided back to England with an infected thumb.

Although the injury did not completely stop Sister Rice from working, it did necessitate a period of rest. While in England Sister Rice continued to work as best she could, at the Middlesex Hospital.

After a medical board held at Millbank on 21 November 1916, Sister Rice was assessed fit and returned to France on 29 November to rejoin 29 Casualty Clearing Station.

Apart from a brief period of leave and another short period of

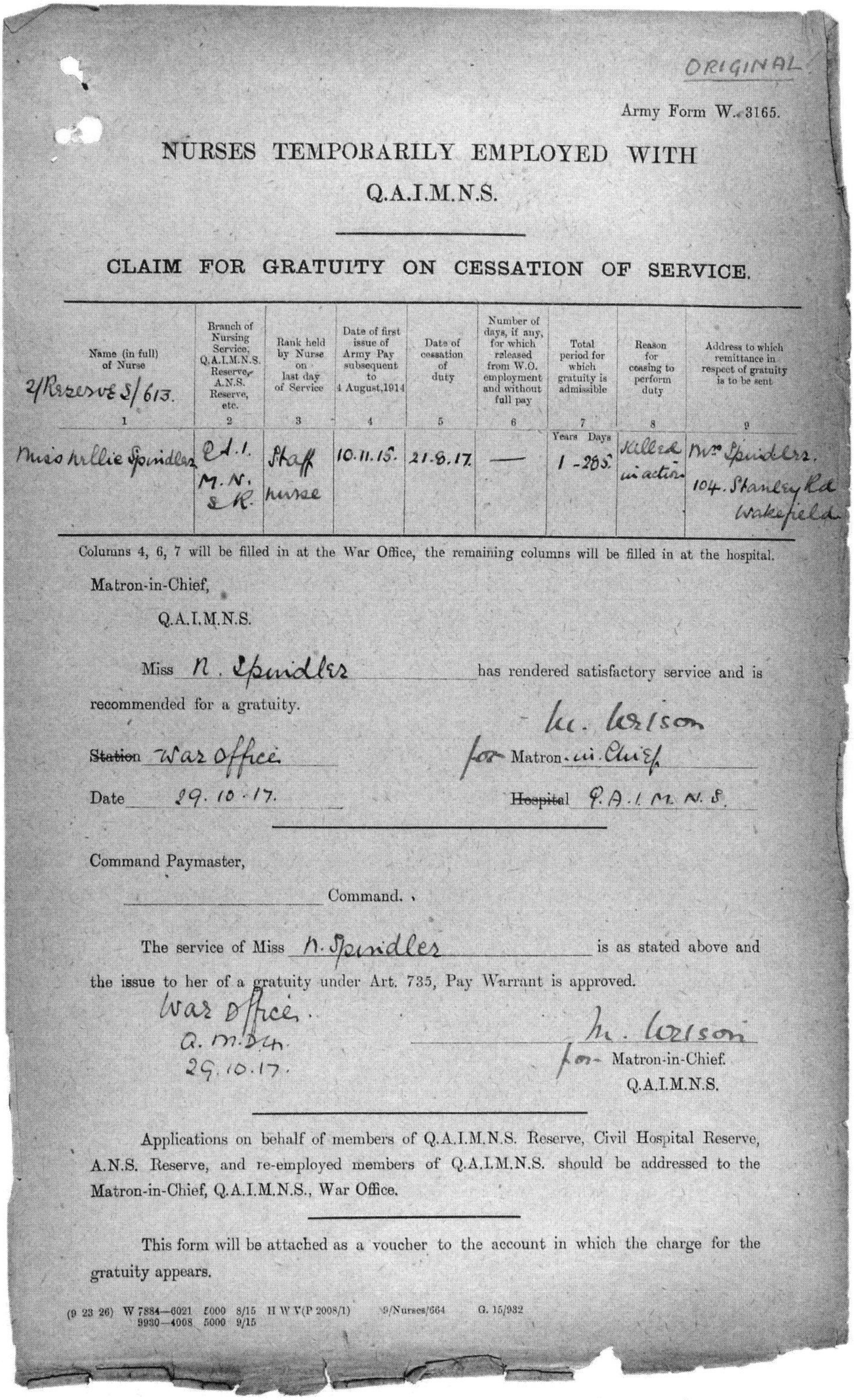

Army Form W.-3165.

NURSES TEMPORARILY EMPLOYED WITH
Q.A.I.M.N.S.

CLAIM FOR GRATUITY ON CESSATION OF SERVICE.

Name (in full) of Nurse	Branch of Nursing Service, Q.A.I.M.N.S. Reserve. A.N.S. Reserve, etc.	Rank held by Nurse on last day of Service	Date of first issue of Army Pay subsequent to 4 August,1914	Date of cessation of duty	Number of days, if any, for which released from W.O. employment and without full pay	Total period for which gratuity is admissible	Reason for ceasing to perform duty	Address to which remittance in respect of gratuity is to be sent
1	2	3	4	5	6	7	8	9
Miss Nellie Spindler	Q.A.I.M.N. S.R.	Staff nurse	10.11.15.	21.8.17.	—	Years Days 1 -285	Killed in action	Mrs Spindler. 104. Stanley Rd Wakefield

2/Reserve S/613.

Columns 4, 6, 7 will be filled in at the War Office, the remaining columns will be filled in at the hospital.

Matron-in-Chief,

    Q.A.I.M.N.S.

    Miss *N. Spindler*   has rendered satisfactory service and is recommended for a gratuity.

Station *War Office*   *M. Wilson* for Matron-in-Chief,

Date *29. 10. 17.*   Hospital *Q.A.I.M.N.S.*

Command Paymaster,

    —————— Command.

    The service of Miss *N. Spindler*   is as stated above and the issue to her of a gratuity under Art. 735, Pay Warrant is approved.

War Office.
A. m.D.4.
29.10.17.

M. Wilson
for Matron-in-Chief.
    Q.A.I.M.N.S.

Applications on behalf of members of Q.A.I.M.N.S. Reserve, Civil Hospital Reserve, A.N.S. Reserve, and re-employed members of Q.A.I.M.N.S. should be addressed to the Matron-in-Chief, Q.A.I.M.N.S., War Office.

This form will be attached as a voucher to the account in which the charge for the gratuity appears.

(9 23 26) W 7884—6021 5000 8/15 H W V(P 2008/1) 9/Nurses/664 G. 15/932
9930—4008 5000 9/15

Fig. 18 *Claim by the mother of Staff Nurse Nellie Spindler for a gratuity for her daughter's service up to the date of her death.* WO 399/7850

sick leave Sister Rice was to remain nursing in France until 15 March 1919.

For her devotion to duty as a nurse Sister Rice was mentioned in despatches and on 3 June 1917 was awarded the Royal Red Cross. The insignia of the RRC was bestowed upon Sister Rice by King George V in early February 1918, and she was photographed coming out of Buckingham Palace after the investiture. The photograph was published in *The Nursing Times* on 16 February 1918.

Nothing is known of Sister Frances Maud Rice after March 1919, when information in her record of service ends.

4.5.2 *Nellie Spindler*
Staff Nurse Nellie Spindler of the Queen Alexandra's Imperial Military Nursing Service (QAIMNS) was one of the few nurses to be killed in action during the First World War.

Born in Wakefield on 10 August 1889, Nellie trained as a nurse at the Township Infirmary in Leeds and she joined QAIMNS on 8 October 1915. Going overseas to France on 23 May 1917, Nellie initially served at 2 General Hospital. Moving to 42 Stationary Hospital in June, Nellie then moved to 44 Casualty Clearing Station at Abbeville on 7 August 1917. Such was the casualty clearing station's proximity to the front line that it was in range of German artillery. At 11 a.m. on the morning of 21 August 1917, the CCS was shelled by the Germans and amongst those wounded was Staff Nurse Spindler. Although her colleagues tried to save her life, Nellie Spindler succumbed to her wounds within an hour of being wounded. According to her record of service, Nellie died at 11.15 a.m.

Staff Nurse Nellie Spindler was buried in Lijssenthoek cemetery. Nellie was 28 years old when she died.

An obituary for Nellie Spindler was published in *The Nursing Times* on 8 September 1917.

Staff Nurse Nellie Spindler's record of service can be found in WO 399/7850.

5 INDIAN ARMY RECORDS OF SERVICE

The majority of records concerning the Indian Army are held by the Asia, Pacific and Africa section of the British Library. The records discussed in this chapter relate primarily to the records held by the National Archives, but also cover the key records of the India Office held by the British Library.

Although the Indian Army was in existence for many years prior to the First World War, rather than cover numerous records, many of which will not necessarily contain data about individuals you may seek, this chapter concentrates on the most significant sources. For those who wish to research Indian Army personnel more fully, the best guide is *Guide to the Records of the India Office Military Department* by Anthony Farrington.

5.1 Officers

Officers in the Indian Army fall into two distinct categories: European officers and Indian officers. Unless otherwise stated, the records discussed in this section relate to European officers only.

During the First World War officers and former officers of the Indian Army saw service not only with their own Army, but also in, rather than just alongside, the British Army. When war broke out in August 1914, there was a large number of serving Indian Army officers in the United Kingdom on leave. There were also many retired Indian Army officers living in the United Kingdom after completing their service. When the war started, many men from these two groups answered their country's call by either helping to fill the shortfall of officers needed in regiments and corps being sent to France, or by becoming officers in many of the new units formed during the war.

To be added to these officers must be those already serving with units in India and those other ranks of the British Army who obtained commissions in the Indian Army at some stage during the war.

5.1.1 Records held by the National Archives

The National Archives has two key record series containing the records of service of officers who saw service during the First World War. The two series, WO 339 and WO 374, are more fully described in chapter 2. However, there are two points that require further elaboration regarding Indian Army officers.

The index of officers' records of service in WO 338 (see 2.2) provides data that needs to be used in order to find a record of service in WO 339. Under the column for regiment or corps, instead of a numerical code for a regiment or an abbreviation for a corps, the abbreviation I.A. representing Indian Army will be found.

The records of service of those British Army other ranks who obtained commissions in the Indian Army between 1914 and 1918 can be found in WO 339/139092–139906 (Long Numbers 289026–289995). In the WO 339 catalogue they are listed at the end, rather than being dispersed throughout the whole record series.

Unfortunately, research into the careers of these particular officers will need to be completed by consulting records held by the National Archives and the British Library, the reason being that the records held by the National Archives contain their other ranks records together with the application papers for a commission and nothing more. Once an individual was commissioned into the Indian Army, records concerning his career were the responsibility of the India Office and not the War Office. Hence the need to use the records at the British Library in the record series L/MIL/9 and L/MIL/14.

5.1.2 Records held by the British Library

Information about accessing the records held by the British Library can be found at 15.3.2.

The series L/MIL/9 and L/MIL/14 consist of a variety of records relating to entry and service in the East India Company and the Indian Army.

Rather than describe all of the records in these series, only information concerning those records likely to contain information about those officers who may have seen service in the First World War will be covered.

Application forms for Queen's Cadetships 1858–1930 containing biographical information about the potential officer can be found in L/MIL/9/292–302.

Indian Army officers who joined as *Indian Army Unattached List* cadets at Sandhurst between 1898 and 1918 are recorded in L/MIL/9/303–311. A list of these cadets for the period 1914–18 is in L/MIL/9/318.

Fig. 19 *Soldiers of the London Rifle Brigade, 5 Battalion (City of London) London Regiment, advancing during the first day of the Battle of Loos, 25 September 1915.*

Between 1915 and 1918, a number of cadets went to the Indian Army colleges at Wellington and Quetta. Details concerning these cadets, their family backgrounds and certificates of age, can be found in L/MIL/9/320–332.

A collection of papers concerning those men granted temporary commissions in the Indian Army or the Indian Army Reserve of Officers may be found in L/MIL/9/435–623. These papers provide basic information about the man, when he was commissioned, which units he served with and when he was released.

Indian Army Statements of Service are preserved in the series L/MIL/14. There is a name index of the papers in this series on the open shelves in the India Office Reading Room in the British Library.

Service Statements for the period 1892–1916 are in the series L/MIL/14/1–49 and they contain printed forms with details about the officer, his service leave and pension.

Information about the promotion of officers can be found in

L/MIL/14/61–76 covering the period 1890–1918.

Many British Army NCOs served on the *Indian Unattached List* in a variety of capacities. Lists of these men can be found in L/MIL/14/144–158 covering the period 1908–22. These lists provide the date of original attestation into the British Army (if applicable), the original unit served in, the Indian Army units served in and any appropriate remarks.

5.2 The *Indian Army List*

The library of the National Archives holds an incomplete run of the *Indian Army List* from 1902 to 1939. In most cases, however, it is possible to find the officer and therefore the information you seek.

The *Indian Army Lists* held in the National Archives Library are similar to the quarterly British *Army List*, in as much as they are published in the same months: January, April, July and October. See 2.6 for further information about the *Army List*.

As with the British *Army List*, the *Indian Army List* contains a name index that provides the relevant page number(s) for each officer who can be found in the list. One useful aspect of the *Indian Army List* over its British equivalent is the amount of information it contains about officers' qualifications. Identified by numerical codes that are listed in the front of each list, most Indian Army Officers were qualified in a diverse range of skills, e.g. languages, unlike many of their British counterparts.

An almost complete set of *Indian Army Lists* is available at the British Library.

5.3 Other Ranks

Unfortunately, very little information about native Indian Army other ranks is available in the United Kingdom. If the individual was awarded a gallantry medal some information may be gained by consulting the appropriate records (see chapter 10). Similarly, some information may be found in the campaign medal records (see chapter 9) and operational records (see chapter 7).

5.4 Case Study

5.4.1 John Hugh McCudden

John Hugh McCudden was born on 31 January 1881 at Gya in Bengal, India, son of Edmund Gerald McCudden and Marion Jane McCudden. He was educated at Rossall School and by W. Arrowsmith, Military Tutor, in Edinburgh, between 1894 and August 1899, when he applied for entry into the Royal Military College by examination. At the time of his application McCudden was living at 18 Grosvenor Crescent, Edinburgh and he stated on his application that he wished to join the infantry.

Commissioned as 2/Lt on 8 January 1901 and appointed to the Indian Army on 7 April 1902, J.H. McCudden joined the 127th Baluch Light Infantry. Having seen operational service in Somaliland between 1908 and 1910, by the time of the First World War he had joined the 21st Prince Albert Victor's Own Cavalry. By the time he was promoted Major in 1916, McCudden was qualified in musketry, the machine-gun and signalling, with certificates in veterinary care, equitation, and linguistic skills in Baluchi, Persian and Pushtu.

Seeing further operational service, this time in Mesopotamia, Major McCudden went on to win the Military Cross in 1916 for 'Conspicuous gallantry when assisting in an attempt to bring in an Indian officer under heavy fire. He also showed great skill and courage when covering a retirement. He had 3 horses shot under him during the day.' The award of the MC was announced in the *London Gazette* on 16 May 1916.

For further service in Mesopotamia, Major McCudden was awarded the DSO and was mentioned in Despatches three times.

Serving on after the war, Major J.H. McCudden DSO, MC was to see further operational service during the third Afghan War of 1919.

Promoted to Brevet Lieutenant Colonel in 1925 and substantive Colonel in 1927, Lieutenant Colonel J.H. McCudden DSO, MC retired on 31 January 1931. According to a letter in private hands, Lieutenant Colonel McCudden did not enjoy a long retirement as he died of a heart attack whilst out riding.

All of the information about Lieutenant Colonel McCudden came from his papers in L/MIL/9 at the British Library, the Indian and British *Army Lists*, the *London Gazette*, WO 100 and some private correspondence.

6 RECORDS OF SERVICE OF THE ROYAL FLYING CORPS AND ROYAL AIR FORCE

Fig. 20 *The crew of a British mobile anti-aircraft gun rush to man their weapon after enemy aircraft are sighted in the Salonika Campaign 1915–18.*

The Royal Flying Corps (RFC) was formed in May 1912 from the Royal Engineers Balloon Section. As a corps of the British Army, the RFC played an important part in the First World War, bringing the use of aircraft from an experimental part of the Army to the forefront of military strategy. The RFC and the naval equivalent, the Royal Naval Air Service (RNAS), were eventually joined together to form the Royal Air Force (RAF), which was created on 1 April 1918.

As the RFC was a corps of the British Army, the records of service of these men should be discussed briefly here. However, the RFC and RAF and all of the records that may be of interest to family

historians are also explored in more detail in *Air Force Records: A Guide for Family Historians* by William Spencer.

6.1   RFC and RAF Officers

RFC and RAF officers are already mentioned in basic terms in 2.5.5. To find an RFC officer's file it is necessary to follow the advice laid down in chapter 2. The records of RAF officers preserved in AIR 76 are arranged in alphabetical order and concern only those officers who had left the RAF by early 1920. The records are very brief and only contain basic biographical data and details of the units in which an individual served.

Unit records concerning the RFC and RAF can be found in the record series AIR 1. At the beginning of the AIR 1 catalogue there is a list of units each with a list of relevant sections within AIR 1 where records may be found. Many of these records include details of officers' service, biographical information and reports concerning their ability.

6.2   RFC Other Ranks

Records of service of RFC airmen can be found in the record series WO 363 and WO 364. See chapter 3 for further information. However, the RFC records in these series only concern men discharged prior to the formation of the RAF on 1 April 1918.

Information concerning the first 1,500 other ranks who joined the RFC can be found in *A Contemptible Little Flying Corps* by I. McInnes and J.V. Webb.

6.3   RAF Other Ranks

Records of men of the RFC who were still serving when the RAF was created, and of those who joined the RAF from 1 April 1918 onwards, can be found in the record series AIR 79. This record series is arranged in service number order. A nominal index that provides the service numbers necessary to use AIR 79, can be found in AIR 78, which is available on microfilm in the National Archives Open Reading Room.

The records in AIR 79 provide basic biographical data, including date and place of birth, physical description, date of enlistment, units served in and medals awarded.

It is also possible to find some information concerning RFC and RAF other ranks in AIR 1.

A list (muster) of all those men serving in the RAF at the time of its formation can be found in AIR 1/819 and AIR 10/237. This muster is arranged in service number order.

6.4 Women's Royal Air Force

There are no records of Women's Royal Air Force (WRAF) officers; they were destroyed a number of years ago.

A small collection of WRAF records are preserved in the record series AIR 80. These records, arranged in alphabetical order, provide basic biographical data, the trade a woman served as and the units she served in.

The records in AIR 80 have been digitized and placed on DocumentsOnline where it is possible to search them by name and download any results.

7 UNIT WAR DIARIES AND OPERATIONAL RECORDS

Prior to the First World War, records kept by individual units to account for their activities during operations varied according to the interests and expertise within that unit. Although the overall commanding officer of an operation produced periodic despatches and reports concerning the conduct of operations, many of which were based on other reports submitted by his subordinate commanders, it was not until 1909 that regulations were created to standardize the way operations were to be reported.

Field Service Regulations (FSR) of 1909 was a two-volume manual that laid down the principles and procedures for how the Army was to conduct operations and to administer itself during the immediate prelude to, and during a war. FSR Part 1 was concerned with operations and FSR Part 2 with the Organization and Administration of the Army.

In FSR Part 2, Chapter XVI, paragraph 140, were laid down rules instructing commanding officers of all units to keep a unit diary when on active operations. The actual wording of these instructions states that the object of a war diary was:

i) To furnish an accurate record of the operations from which the history of the war can subsequently be prepared.

ii) To collect information for future reference with a view to effecting improvements in the organization, education, training, equipment and administration of the army for war.

7.1 Army Structures

During the First World War, the British Army expanded from a small pre-war regular army into a huge fighting machine. In order to find a specific unit war diary it helps to understand how the Army was arranged. The easiest way to explain the arrangement is to look at the British Expeditionary Force in France and Flanders.

At the head of the whole Army overseas in France was the

Commander in Chief (C in C), initially Sir John French, but from December 1915 until the end of the war Field Marshal Sir Douglas Haig. Below the Commander in Chief the structure was as follows:

Army
Corps
Division
Brigade
Battalion or Equivalent

When listed, armies are usually numbered I–V; corps are also numbered using Roman numerals; divisions are listed in Arabic numerals 1–75 and brigades are similarly numbered. Infantry battalions are listed using Arabic numerals, e.g. 2 Battalion or 1/4 Battalion. For more information about the numbering of regiments, see *Your Country Needs You* by Martin Middlebrook.

Although the units within this chain of command could and did change, this was the basic hierarchy of the Army overseas. In this hierarchy there are a number of constants. Until the spring of 1918, there were always four infantry battalions in a brigade. This figure was reduced to three battalions per brigade due to manpower shortages, when many infantry battalions were disbanded and the manpower redistributed amongst other units, mostly in the same brigade if not division.

Apart from the units listed under a specific division and brigades, many units served as either army or corps troops, directly controlled by the commanders of the relevant army or corps, rather than under divisional or brigade command.

Most divisions consisted of a collection of divisional troops, answerable to and controlled directly by divisional headquarters. These troops were the artillery and other support troops (medical, supply and signals) that supported the three infantry brigades. The three infantry brigades each had their own brigade commander who was subordinate to the divisional commander but superior to each infantry battalion commander. Although a brigade could act fairly independently in minor operations, most of the time it was controlled by the divisional commander.

An infantry battalion, with a lieutenant colonel in command, was split into a number of companies, usually identified by a letter. Most battalions were split into an HQ Company and four other companies, usually A–D. Each company was usually commanded by a captain, although during operations where casualties were sustained command would devolve down to the next most senior individual. Each company was further broken down, firstly into platoons, commanded by a

Fig. 21 *A retrospective report on operations carried out by 17 Battalion Sherwood Foresters in September 1916 contained in the unit war diary.*
WO 95/2587

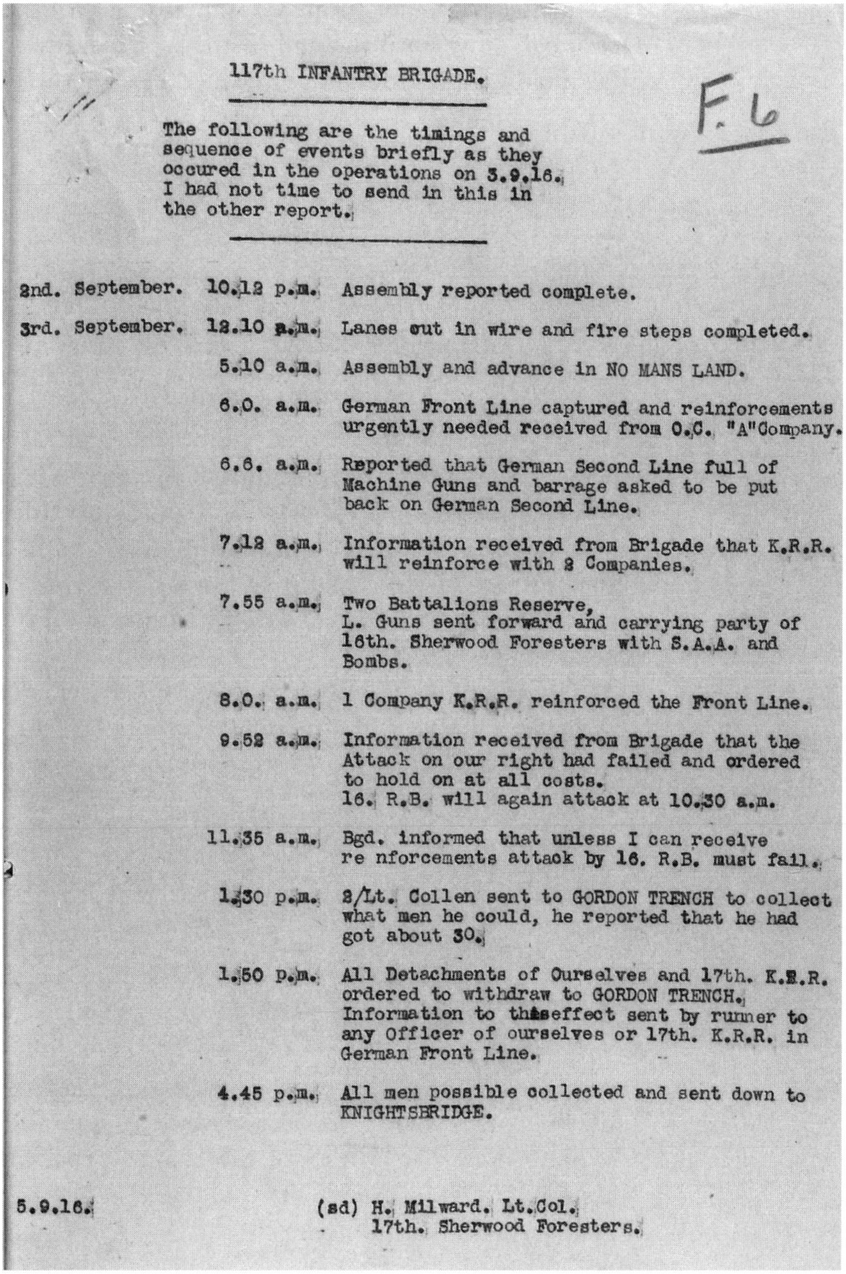

117th INFANTRY BRIGADE.

The following are the timings and sequence of events briefly as they occured in the operations on 3.9.16. I had not time to send in this in the other report.

F.6

2nd. September.	10.12 p.m.	Assembly reported complete.
3rd. September.	12.10 a.m.	Lanes out in wire and fire steps completed.
	5.10 a.m.	Assembly and advance in NO MANS LAND.
	6.0. a.m.	German Front Line captured and reinforcements urgently needed received from O.C. "A"Company.
	6.6. a.m.	Reported that German Second Line full of Machine Guns and barrage asked to be put back on German Second Line.
	7.12 a.m.	Information received from Brigade that K.R.R. will reinforce with 2 Companies.
	7.55 a.m.	Two Battalions Reserve, L. Guns sent forward and carrying party of 16th. Sherwood Foresters with S.A.A. and Bombs.
	8.0. a.m.	1 Company K.R.R. reinforced the Front Line.
	9.52 a.m.	Information received from Brigade that the Attack on our right had failed and ordered to hold on at all costs. 16. R.B. will again attack at 10.30 a.m.
	11.35 a.m.	Bgd. informed that unless I can receive reinforcements attack by 16. R.B. must fail.
	1.30 p.m.	2/Lt. Collen sent to GORDON TRENCH to collect what men he could, he reported that he had got about 30.
	1.50 p.m.	All Detachments of Ourselves and 17th. K.R.R. ordered to withdraw to GORDON TRENCH. Information to this effect sent by runner to any Officer of ourselves or 17th. K.R.R. in German Front Line.
	4.45 p.m.	All men possible collected and sent down to KNIGHTSBRIDGE.

5.9.16.

(sd) H. Milward. Lt.Col.
17th. Sherwood Foresters.

lieutenant or second lieutenant, and then into sections commanded by a sergeant or corporal.

Different parts of the Army had different titles for their units. In cavalry regiments the equivalent of the infantry company was the squadron and below that the troop. The artillery was usually in brigades and then batteries. Both the Royal Engineers and the

Army Service Corps were arranged by company.

If you know the full title of the part of the Army for which you require a unit war diary, you can use that title to do a keyword search on the Catalogue.

The arrangement of the British Expeditionary Force (BEF) during the war can be found in *History of The Great War: Orders of Battle*, by A.F. Becke. Known as the 'Orders of Battle', this work lists all units serving in an army, corps or division. A copy of this work can be found behind the staff desk in the Open Reading Room. The composition of the BEF at certain times during the war can also be found in the *Official History of the Great War*, a copy of which is available in the National Archives Library. Orders of battle can also be found in WO 95/5467–87.

Beyond the Western Front, the organization of the British Army in other operational theatres varied according to the size of the force in that theatre. In the case of forces in Egypt and Gallipoli, they had Expeditionary Force commanders and then a number of corps under their command. Under the corps were the divisions and brigades and associated troops.

When consulting the paper copy of the WO 95 catalogue, at the heading of each section (operational theatre) of the catalogue will be found the diaries of the highest level of the command structure, followed by the subordinate organizations and units.

7.2 Unit War Diaries (WO 95)

The diaries found in the record series WO 95 comprise over 10,000 individual unit diaries covering all operational theatres in which the British Army saw service. Diaries for dominion forces which served as part of the British Army can be found in WO 95, as can those of the Indian Army. Not only do the diaries cover operations between 1914 and 1918, they also cover operations up to 1920, including those in Russia and India.

The diaries are arranged by operational theatre and then in a hierarchical order, starting at General Headquarters and then sorted by armies, corps, divisions, brigades and then battalions. Although this is the basic chain of command, the arrangement of the catalogue can alter depending on the operational theatre.

UNIT WAR DIARY OPERATIONAL THEATRES

| I | France and Flanders |
| II | Italy |

WAR DIARY

~~INTELLIGENCE SUMMARY~~
(Erase heading not required.)

Instructions regarding War Diaries and Intelligence Summaries are contained in F. S. Regs., Part II. and the Staff Manual respectively. Title pages will be prepared in manuscript.

28th (COUNTY OF LONDON) BATTALION LONDON REGT.
No. ....
Date 1 NOV 1917
ORDERLY ROOM
(ARTISTS RIFLES)

Army Form C. 2118.

Place	Date	Hour	Summary of Events and Information	Remarks and references to Appendices
REIGERSBERG CAMP	28.10.17		Battalion went into the line. H.Q. at ALBATROSS FARM taking over from NELSON Battalion.	
ALBATROSS FARM C.2 & 2.3	29.10.17		On the line.	
	30.10.17	5.50 am	Battalion attacked	
	31.10.17	7.30 pm	Relieved by NELSON Battalion & returned to IRISH FARM. Total estimated casualties for the period 28th - 31st. Officers: killed 6. Wounded 4. O.R. 70. 130 Missing 124	

A6945 Wt. W11422/M1160 350,000 12/16 D. D. & L. Forms/C./2118/14.

Fig. 22 *Unit war diary for 28 Battalion London Regiment. Between 28 and 31 October the Battalion had 334 casualties and yet the diary is brief.* WO 95/3119

III	Gallipoli and Dardanelles
IV	Egypt, Palestine and Syria
V	Salonika, Macedonia, Turkey, Black Sea, Caucasus and South Russia
VI	Mesopotamia, Iraq and North Russia
VII	East Africa, West Africa and Cameroon
VIII	India and East Persia
IX	North Persia and Siberia
X	Colonies: Aden, Bermuda, Ceylon, Hong Kong, North China, Gibraltar, Malta, Mauritius, Singapore
XI	Home Forces

If you are looking for a specific unit diary, there are a number of routes open to you to locate it.

Apart from using the printed WO 95 catalogue to find unit diaries, it is possible to locate them by doing a keyword search on the Catalogue. By placing the unit name in the top field of the search page and WO 95 in the last field it is possible to list all diaries for each unit. As many units saw service in more than one operational theatre, and in many cases in more than one division, by using the Catalogue the problem of locating all of the relevant diaries is reduced.

Many of the unit war diaries in WO 95 have now been digitized and placed on DocumentsOnline. If you try to order a WO 95 on the

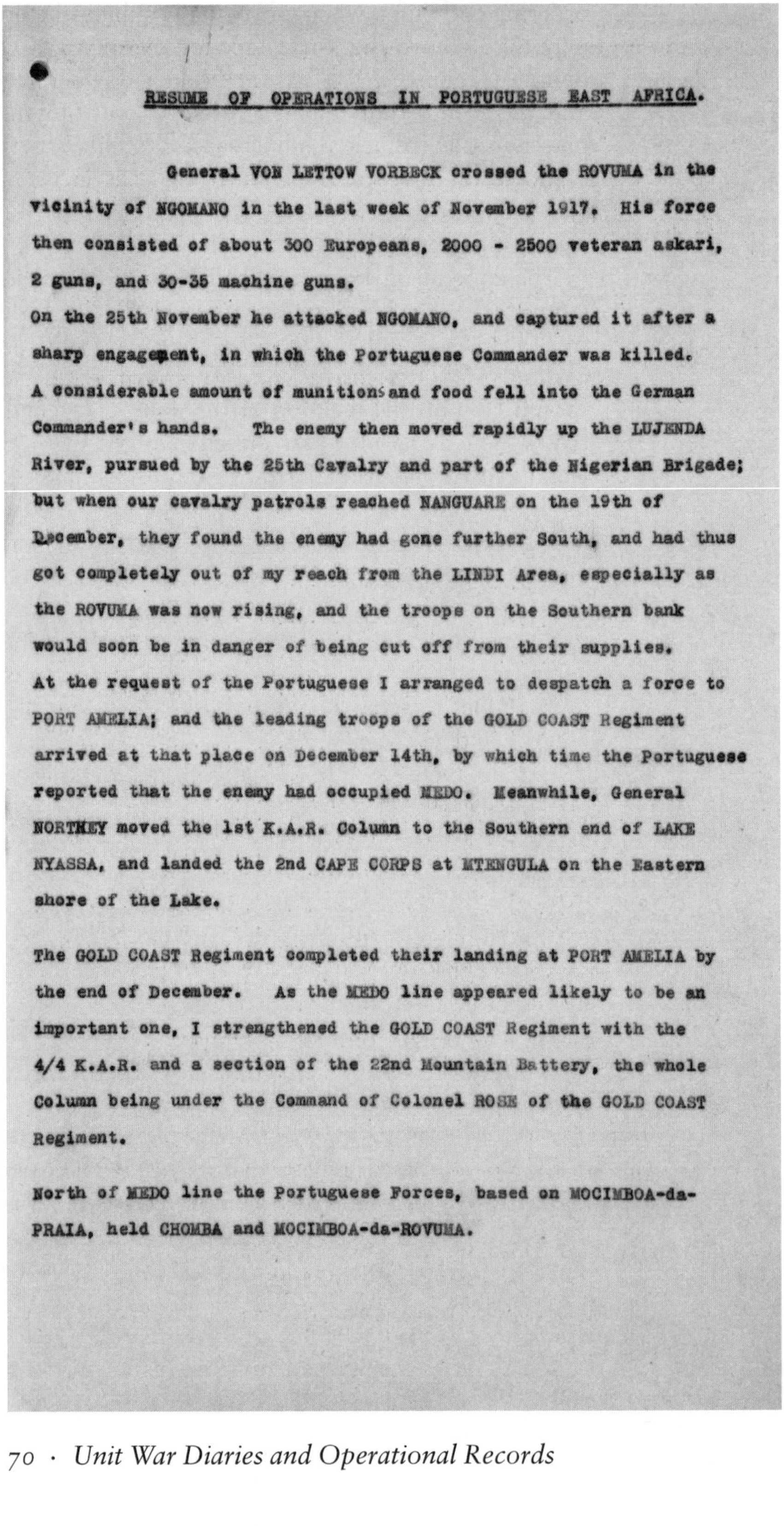

RESUME OF OPERATIONS IN PORTUGUESE EAST AFRICA.

General VON LETTOW VORBECK crossed the ROVUMA in the vicinity of NGOMANO in the last week of November 1917. His force then consisted of about 300 Europeans, 2000 - 2500 veteran askari, 2 guns, and 30-35 machine guns.

On the 25th November he attacked NGOMANO, and captured it after a sharp engagement, in which the Portuguese Commander was killed. A considerable amount of munitions and food fell into the German Commander's hands. The enemy then moved rapidly up the LUJENDA River, pursued by the 25th Cavalry and part of the Nigerian Brigade; but when our cavalry patrols reached NANGUARE on the 19th of December, they found the enemy had gone further South, and had thus got completely out of my reach from the LINDI Area, especially as the ROVUMA was now rising, and the troops on the Southern bank would soon be in danger of being cut off from their supplies.

At the request of the Portuguese I arranged to despatch a force to PORT AMELIA; and the leading troops of the GOLD COAST Regiment arrived at that place on December 14th, by which time the Portuguese reported that the enemy had occupied MEDO. Meanwhile, General NORTHEY moved the 1st K.A.R. Column to the Southern end of LAKE NYASSA, and landed the 2nd CAPE CORPS at MTENGULA on the Eastern shore of the Lake.

The GOLD COAST Regiment completed their landing at PORT AMELIA by the end of December. As the MEDO line appeared likely to be an important one, I strengthened the GOLD COAST Regiment with the 4/4 K.A.R. and a section of the 22nd Mountain Battery, the whole Column being under the Command of Colonel ROSE of the GOLD COAST Regiment.

North of MEDO line the Portuguese Forces, based on MOCIMBOA-da-PRAIA, held CHOMBA and MOCIMBOA-da-ROVUMA.

Fig. 23 *Report of British Army operations in Portuguese East Africa in 1917 and 1918.* WO 158/476

ordering computer, when you actually submit the order the computer may take you to the direct link for the digitized copy. Most of the digitized copies of WO 95 are broken down into individual units, and those into individual months. As with anything digitized and placed on DocumentsOnline, access is free to those visiting the National Archives at Kew, but you will incur a charge to print anything. For those accessing WO 95 externally, you will have to pay to download anything.

The content of the unit war diary varies according to the level of interest that the compiler of the diary had in the task. In many cases it was the responsibility of the adjutant to compile the diary from information provided by a number of sources. In basic terms the diary should contain the location of the unit, its strength and any occurrences which the unit was either involved in or which affected it. Details of all operational action either by or against a unit and information about personnel, including casualties, are usually shown. Also found in most unit war diaries are operational orders from higher authority, maps and plans. Many of these are usually listed as appendixes at the end of each month. In most diaries only officers are mentioned by name but, depending upon the interest shown by the compiler, other ranks may be mentioned.

Examples of typical data found in a unit war diary can be seen in Figs. 21 and 22.

Unit war diaries can provide useful contextual information about operations, especially concerning honours and awards granted for deeds performed during those operations. Beyond published regimental histories and numerous personal accounts, the unit diaries are the only other records that can provide a picture of what really happened on a day-to-day basis.

Unit war diaries for the 63rd (Royal Naval) Division can be found in WO 95 and also in ADM 137/3063–88.

7.3 War Diary Extracts in WO 154

A number of items of a sensitive nature were removed from the diaries in WO 95. These extracts mostly concerned disciplinary matters, many of which resulted in an execution. WO 154 is arranged by unit in a similar way to WO 95 and can be searched by unit on the Catalogue.

7.4 Military Headquarters Papers and Correspondence (WO 158)

Arranged by operational theatre and then by unit down to brigade level, these records are the papers created by various units and describe in more detail than most unit war diaries numerous operations undertaken during the war. Although individuals are sometimes mentioned, especially in those papers for operational theatres other than France and Flanders, the majority of information in these files concerns the conduct of operations and the planning that took place beforehand.

7.5 Intelligence Summaries (WO 157)

Whilst not providing information about individuals, the intelligence summaries in WO 157 do provide information about who was opposing the units sending in the report, together with information about other events at the front. These summaries are arranged by operational theatre and by unit, usually no lower than brigade.

7.6 War Office Registered Files: General Series (WO 32)

A number of operational reports by several different commanders can be found in WO 32. Many of the files concern operations in Africa but there is also a report concerning the seizure of Tsingtau, the German colony in China, in 1914.

To identify material in WO 32 you can search the Catalogue using keywords, of which the following may of use:

> Place names (such as Cameroon or East Africa, for example)
> Senior commanders' names (usually the author of despatches)
> Operation(s)
> Despatch(es)

Fig. 24 (facing)
Report on the Medical Services during operations in Cameroon from September 1914–February 1916.
WO 32/5327

The arrangement of WO 32 is by subject code, but by keyword searching on the Catalogue you should avoid the need to use the paper catalogue. However, the code in WO 32 for the various countries in which the British Army fought is always prefixed with 'O' for overseas and then with another letter for the given country.

REPORT ON THE WORK OF THE MEDICAL SERVICE IN THE

CAMEROONS, September 1914 to February 1916.

CLIMATE.

1.   This campaign was fought under somewhat unusual
conditions as it was conducted in a very unhealthy
tropical country, and yet organised on a large scale.

It involved a high sick rate with the dangers
of serious epidemics which could have interfered with
operations, yet for military and other reasons the
campaign had to be medically self contained.

The military reasons were the difficulty of
obtaining reinforcements and the need of retaining
and returning to the ranks every European and native
fighting man.

The medical reasons were the absence of large
hospitals and medical staffs in the British West
African Colonies to which patients might have
otherwise been sent, and that of hospital ships
which could have transported really ill and badly
wounded patients.

2.   The charts of altitude, rainfall, health areas,
and vegetation (Tables 1 to 4) show that the region
in which the Columns were compelled, for the most
part, to operate was peculiarly unfavourable for the
employment of large bodies of troops.   This coastal
area of a tropical country, with its great rainfall,
low altitude, and dense vegetation was notoriously
very unhealthy.

The moist hot atmosphere of this area was very
enervating to Europeans, and the want of supplies in
the forest region prevented the troops obtaining all
the fresh food necessary for health.

The Columns under General Cunliffe and the
northern portion of General Aymerich's eastern
Columns, operating in healthy country, usually with
plentiful food supplies, were much more favourable
situated, and only the southern portion of General
Aymerich's troops were subjected to conditions at
all comparable with those which rendered the sick
rate in our Columns so high.

MEDICAL STAFF.

3.   The medical service of the expedition was
organised under unusual conditions as its units were
hurriedly created at sea, before the troops could
land, from a personnel mainly civilian, and materiel
and equipment of various nature.

Two Royal Army Medical Corps Officers, 26
doctors of the West African Medical Service, 6 Nursing
Sisters, 4 Non-Commissioned Officers, and 20 Dressers

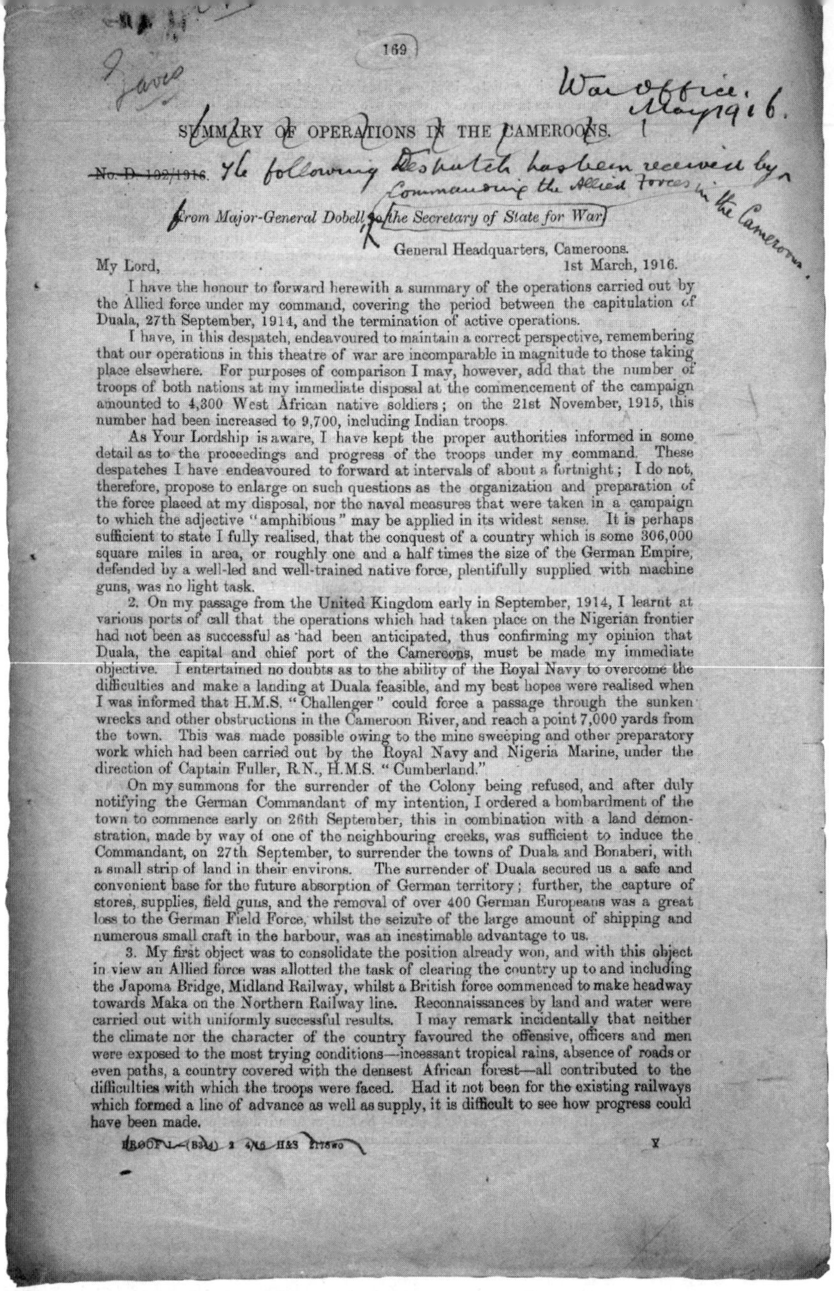

169

War Office. May 1916.

SUMMARY OF OPERATIONS IN THE CAMEROONS.

~~No. D 102/1916.~~ The following Despatch has been received by ~~from Major-General Dobell~~ ~~to the Secretary of State for War~~ Commanding the Allied Forces in the Cameroons.

From Major-General Dobell to the Secretary of State for War.

General Headquarters, Cameroons.
1st March, 1916.

My Lord,

I have the honour to forward herewith a summary of the operations carried out by the Allied force under my command, covering the period between the capitulation of Duala, 27th September, 1914, and the termination of active operations.

I have, in this despatch, endeavoured to maintain a correct perspective, remembering that our operations in this theatre of war are incomparable in magnitude to those taking place elsewhere. For purposes of comparison I may, however, add that the number of troops of both nations at my immediate disposal at the commencement of the campaign amounted to 4,300 West African native soldiers; on the 21st November, 1915, this number had been increased to 9,700, including Indian troops.

As Your Lordship is aware, I have kept the proper authorities informed in some detail as to the proceedings and progress of the troops under my command. These despatches I have endeavoured to forward at intervals of about a fortnight; I do not, therefore, propose to enlarge on such questions as the organization and preparation of the force placed at my disposal, nor the naval measures that were taken in a campaign to which the adjective "amphibious" may be applied in its widest sense. It is perhaps sufficient to state I fully realised, that the conquest of a country which is some 306,000 square miles in area, or roughly one and a half times the size of the German Empire, defended by a well-led and well-trained native force, plentifully supplied with machine guns, was no light task.

2. On my passage from the United Kingdom early in September, 1914, I learnt at various ports of call that the operations which had taken place on the Nigerian frontier had not been as successful as had been anticipated, thus confirming my opinion that Duala, the capital and chief port of the Cameroons, must be made my immediate objective. I entertained no doubts as to the ability of the Royal Navy to overcome the difficulties and make a landing at Duala feasible, and my best hopes were realised when I was informed that H.M.S. "Challenger" could force a passage through the sunken wrecks and other obstructions in the Cameroon River, and reach a point 7,000 yards from the town. This was made possible owing to the mine sweeping and other preparatory work which had been carried out by the Royal Navy and Nigeria Marine, under the direction of Captain Fuller, R.N., H.M.S. "Cumberland."

On my summons for the surrender of the Colony being refused, and after duly notifying the German Commandant of my intention, I ordered a bombardment of the town to commence early on 26th September, this in combination with a land demonstration, made by way of one of the neighbouring creeks, was sufficient to induce the Commandant, on 27th September, to surrender the towns of Duala and Bonaberi, with a small strip of land in their environs. The surrender of Duala secured us a safe and convenient base for the future absorption of German territory; further, the capture of stores, supplies, field guns, and the removal of over 400 German Europeans was a great loss to the German Field Force, whilst the seizure of the large amount of shipping and numerous small craft in the harbour, was an inestimable advantage to us.

3. My first object was to consolidate the position already won, and with this object in view an Allied force was allotted the task of clearing the country up to and including the Japoma Bridge, Midland Railway, whilst a British force commenced to make headway towards Maka on the Northern Railway line. Reconnaissances by land and water were carried out with uniformly successful results. I may remark incidentally that neither the climate nor the character of the country favoured the offensive, officers and men were exposed to the most trying conditions—incessant tropical rains, absence of roads or even paths, a country covered with the densest African forest—all contributed to the difficulties with which the troops were faced. Had it not been for the existing railways which formed a line of advance as well as supply, it is difficult to see how progress could have been made.

Y

Fig. 25 *Draft despatch from Major General Dobell on operations in Cameroon.* WO 32/5327

7.7 War Office Directorate of Military Operations (WO 106)

Various reports concerning operations in certain parts of the world during the First World War can be found in WO 106. Amongst the records in WO 106 are files concerning operations in the following places:

WO 106/571–89	German South West Africa
WO 106/257, 580, 582 and 585	East Africa
WO 106/1533	Togoland

WO 106/638–56	Cameroon
WO 106/660–8	Tsingtau
WO 106/1490	Contains a history of the British East African Expeditionary Force

7.8 The Official Historian's Papers

The key source material used by the Official Historian for the creation of the published official histories were the unit war diaries in WO 95, the papers in WO 157 and WO 158 and the maps in WO 153 and WO 297. The historian's papers are, however, not be overlooked as they contain the personal diaries of a number of individuals who participated in the war, together with working drafts and comments in the form of letters on those drafts. Many of the letters and diaries are catalogued by name of the author and other letters are listed under the headings of each volume of the official history. The Official Historian's papers can be found in CAB 44 and CAB 45.

7.9 Printed Sources

Many of the operational records discussed in this chapter were used by the Cabinet Historical Section to produce the *Official History*. Written after the war, many of the volumes of the *Official History* were not published until the 1940s. Some volumes were only produced in draft and were therefore never published. The volumes of the *Official History* that were published are available in the National Archives Library. Arranged by operational theatre, these histories can provide much useful information about the various battles fought around the world. Included in these histories are numerous maps.

A number of draft volumes of the *Official History*, most notably East Africa volume 2, can be found in CAB 44/4–10 and comments and compilations of data on the same volume can be found CAB 45/60–74.

Although not based solely on primary sources, the *Battleground Europe* series of books published by Leo Cooper are an excellent source of contextual information for the battles each volume covers. Many of these guides include illustrations of the areas they cover, including contemporary and modern photographs.

The *British Battalion* series of books by Ray Westlake and published by Leo Cooper provide a very useful synopsis of the war

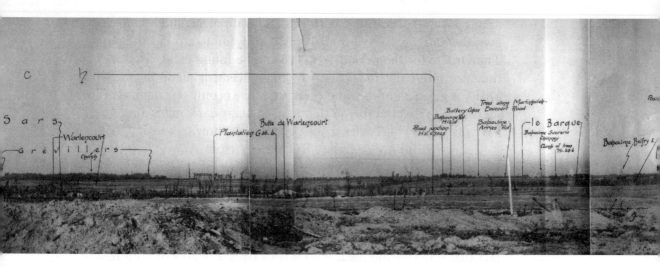

Fig. 26 *Panoramic photograph showing the front line at Butte de Warlencourt on the Somme.* WO 316/39

diaries of those infantry regiments that took part in operations in France and Belgium in 1914 and the first half of 1915, at Gallipoli or on the Somme in 1916.

7.10 Embarkation and Disembarkation Records

From information contained on the medal index cards (see 9.2), it is possible to know when an individual first sailed for service overseas. By using the date and applying it to a number of different sources, it is possible to identify the unit(s) that left Britain on that date.

The embarkation and disembarkation records list those units that sailed from or to Britain on specific dates, together with the number of men of a given unit leaving or returning. They can be found in WO 25/3533–86 (leaving) and WO 25/3696–3746 (returning).

Two other records that can provide the dates when units sailed overseas can be found in WO 379/16 and WO 162/7.

The dates upon which all of the infantry and cavalry regiments left the United Kingdom can be found in *British Regiments 1914–1918* by E.A. James.

7.11 Army Orders

In the record series WO 123 can be found a number of different types of Administrative Orders. These Orders must not be confused with the Operational Orders that can be found in WO 95 and WO 158.

Army Orders were the mechanism used to disseminate information about pay and conditions, uniforms and equipment, and honours and awards, and were sent to all British Army units around the world. The Orders for the period 1914–18 can be found in WO 123/56–60; they are internally indexed. Any announcement made in an Army Order is given a number and therefore there is only one item of information with that number in that year. In many cases items announced in Army Orders may refer to an Order from a previous year.

General Routine Orders (GROs) differ from Army Orders in as much as they are specific to a given operational theatre and the information they contain is more pertinent to the operational theatre than to the British Army as a whole.

The information contained in GROs varies from theatre to theatre. In most theatres they contain information about courts martial (the fact that one is being held, who it is to try and who will hold it, and the results of any trials, especially if the death sentence was passed), equipment and in many cases messages from high command to the whole army in a given theatre. Other information found in these Orders may vary. In the GROs for East Africa and also for Mesopotamia, information about officers' appointments, promotions and resignations may also be found.

GROs for the First World War period can be found under the following references:

Theatre	Reference
France	WO 123/199–203
Italy	WO 123/279
Egypt	WO 123/280–2
East Africa	WO 123/288–9
Mesopotamia	WO 123/290
Salonika	WO 123/293

7.12 Photographs

Apart from occasions where isolated photographs turn up in odd places, the National Archives has very few dedicated records series solely for photographs. There are, however, a number of small collections of photographs that are mostly panoramas of the various front lines (see Fig. 26). The following record series may be of interest:

WO 316	Western Front	1914–18
WO 317	Gallipoli	1915–19
WO 319	Palestine	1916–18
WO 323	Italy	1916–18

8   TRENCH AND OTHER MAPS

During the First World War tens of thousands of maps were produced for use at or near the front line. Many maps were based upon work carried out by Belgian or French surveyors. However, the majority of maps used during the war were produced by the survey sections of the Royal Engineers, the Geographical Section General Staff (GSGS). Although many of the maps were produced using traditional surveying methods, much of the detail added to maps during the war was based on aerial reconnaissance photographs taken by the RFC and RAF.

In the National Archives are preserved over 10,000 maps showing the disposition of both British and German forces in various places and at various times throughout the war.

8.1   Trench Maps

The collections of trench maps preserved in the National Archives are arranged by operational theatre, then by scale and then in sheet number order. The following record series contain trench maps:

WO 297	Western Front
WO 298	Salonika
WO 300	German South West and German East Africa
WO 301	Gallipoli
WO 302	Mesopotamia
WO 303	Palestine
WO 369	Italy

Depending upon the date and scale, the amount of information contained on the map may vary. Although the description of each map in the catalogue will tell you its effective date and whether it shows the Allied (A) or German (G) lines, it is sometimes only possible to find a map that shows the area you may be interested in either before or after the exact date you require.

Most of the trench maps are for the war from 1915 onwards, with

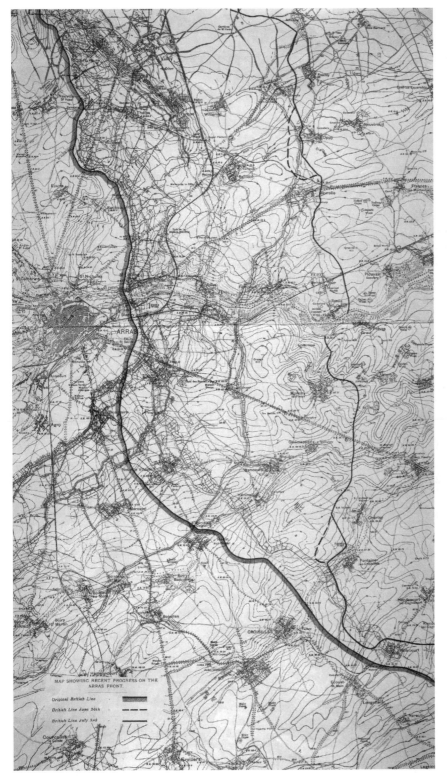

Fig. 27 *Trench map showing the advances made during the battle around Arras in 1917.*
WO 297/5941

Trench and Other Maps · 79

Fig. 28 *Military Headquarters map, showing very detailed locations of units taking part in the Battle of Loos on 25 September 1915.* WO 153/145

most being later than that. If you are unable to find a map in one of the trench map record series, you may need to look in WO 153 or see if one is preserved in the unit war diary.

There were a variety of different scales used on maps in the First World War. However, although there are many maps of the 1:5000 scale which can be very detailed, the majority preserved in the National Archives are in 1:10000 and 1:20000, which still provide enough information for most uses.

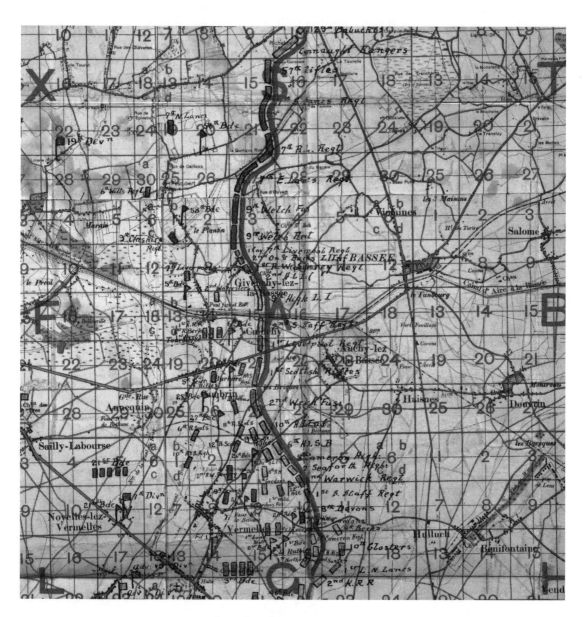

8.2 How to Use Trench Maps

There is a brief guide to using trench maps available at the staff desks in the Open Reading Room and the Map and Large Document Reading Room at the National Archives. It is recommended that you use this guide to find all maps in WO 297 and to work out any particular grid reference.

Each area of France and Belgium was given a number, which was further split into NW, NE, SW and SE. Each of these four sheets can be further divided into four sheets numbered 1–4. A further division by letter and then number will eventually mean that you will be able to work out any given position in a box 1000 yards by 1000 yards.

Index maps that tell you what number was given to a particular area are available at the beginning of the WO 297 catalogue and at the back of the 'First World War, 1914–1918: Military Maps' leaflet.

If you know the number and geographical part of a given sheet, e.g. 28 NW, you can use that data to do a keyword search on the Catalogue.

What follows is an example of using a grid reference found in a unit war diary.

According to the diary of 18 Division for July 1917 (WO 95/2016), the division was occupying positions shown on 1:20000 sheets 28 NW/NE. The specific grid reference where 7 Battalion, Queen's Royal West Surrey Regiment were in July 1917 was 123a58.40. This translates to Sheet 28 NW 3, Box I, Box a, grid 58.40. The closest map to the date 10 July 1917, when 2nd Lieutenant/Acting Captain H.J. A'Bear (see 2.10.1) was killed, is WO 297/701.

8.3 Military Headquarters Maps (WO 153)

Most trench maps were not allowed too close to the front line as the data contained on them could be of use to the enemy should the position be captured.

Detailed maps maintained by brigade, division, corps and army headquarters, showing dispositions of troops, enemy artillery positions, planning and progress of offensive operations are in WO 153. Many of the maps can be found using the online Catalogue by searching using a place name, unit identity and date. As many of these maps were kept by high command, it is possible to find maps showing exact unit positions rather than working out a position from a grid reference. An example of an annotated map can be seen in Fig. 28.

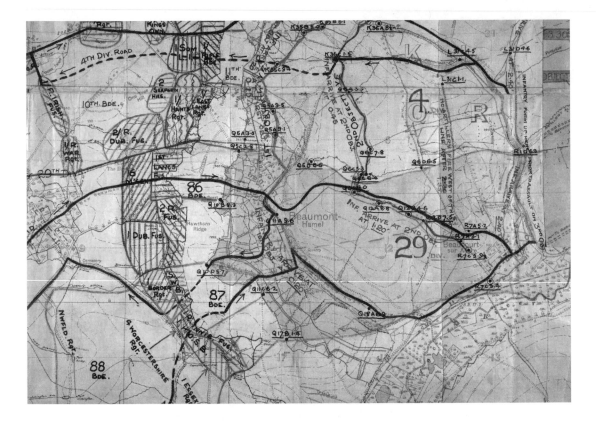

8.4   Other Maps

Fig. 29 *First day objectives for the Battle of the Somme, 1 July 1916. It took many weeks to get to the point at which the infantry was to form up to attack the 3rd objective (on right hand side of the map).* WO 153/167

There are a wide variety of different map record series. WO 78 is the key pre-First World War record series. Maps showing operations in West and East Africa can be found in CO 700. The maps used and created by the Foreign Office can be found in the series FO 925.

There are basic maps in the *Official Histories*, but compared with the maps in WO 153, for example, they lack detail.

A number of trench maps on CD-ROM based on records held by the Imperial War Museum and the National Archives have been produced by the Naval and Military Press.

It is possible to search all of the above-mentioned series by place name or keyword on the Catalogue.

9 CAMPAIGN MEDALS

Six different campaign medals were awarded for service during the First World War and, apart from exceptional cases, the maximum number of these medals that could be awarded to one man or woman was three. The exceptions to the rule were those individuals who served in the Merchant Navy, either before, or in some cases after, serving in the Army, and who received the Mercantile Marine War Medal. This precluded recipients from receiving the Victory Medal, although many did actually receive it!

Many men and women who were discharged from the Army as a result of sickness or wounds contracted or received during the war were awarded a specific badge called the Silver War Badge. The records concerning these badges can be found with the campaign medal records. A Silver War Badge is shown in Fig. 30.

All campaign medals issued for service during the war were named, either on the back (the reverse) in the case of the two stars, or around the edge in the case of the circular medals. For other ranks, the naming on all medals includes name, rank, number and regiment or corps. In the case of the 1914 Star, the naming also includes the battalion of the regiment. For officers, apart from on the 1914 Star and 1914/15 Star where the unit is given, only rank and name are given on the British War Medal and Victory Medal.

The campaign medals awarded for service during the war were issued from 1919 onwards. Medals won by other ranks were sent automatically, as were those won by individuals who were no longer living. Officers had to apply for their campaign medals, which is one reason why it is possible to find the medal index card for a missing officer—he never applied.

For further information about the campaign medals awarded during the period 1914–18, see *British Battles and Medals* by D. Birch, J. Hayward and R. Bishop.

In order to see which medal(s) an individual was eligible for, each man had a medal record card. This card, an Army Form W 5103, was double-sided. One side was used for the 1914 Star and 1914/15 Star and the other side for the British War Medal and Victory Medal. The Medal Record Card recorded the name, rank and number of a soldier, the highest rank they held for at least six months, the operational theatre(s) they served in and the date(s) they served in each theatre. If a man changed battalions with a given regiment, that would be recorded in the same way as a complete change from one regiment or corps to another.

Once the card was completed, it would be possible to work out an individual's medal entitlement and how the medals should be named.

9.1 Medals and Silver War Badge

The 1914 Star, authorized in 1917, was awarded to those military personnel and some civilians who saw service in France and Belgium between 5 August and 22 November 1914. In 1919 a bar with the inscription '5th Aug–22nd Nov' was sanctioned. Only those personnel who had actually been under fire during the specified dates on the bar were eligible. This medal should always be accompanied by a British War Medal and a Victory Medal.

The 1914/15 Star, authorized in 1918, was awarded to those service personnel and civilians who saw service in France and Belgium from 23 November 1914 to 31 December 1915, and to those individuals who saw service in any other operational theatre, apart from France and Belgium, between 5 August 1914 and 31 December 1915. These other operational theatres are listed in section 9.5, but included East and West Africa, Gallipoli and Egypt. This medal should always be accompanied by a British War Medal and a Victory Medal.

The British War Medal 1914–20, authorized in 1919, was awarded to eligible service personnel and civilians alike. Qualification for the award varied slightly depending on which service the individual was in. The basic requirement for Army personnel was that they either entered a theatre of war or rendered approved service overseas between 5 August 1914 and 11 November 1918. Service in Russia between 1919 and 1920 also qualified for the award. This medal could be awarded on its own.

The Victory Medal 1914–19 was also authorized in 1919 and was awarded to those eligible personnel who served on the establishment of a unit in an operational theatre. The Victory Medal should always be accompanied by at least a British War Medal.

The Territorial Force War Medal 1914–19 was awarded to members of the Territorial Force only. To qualify for the award the

Fig. 30 *A Silver War Badge.*

recipient had to have been a member of the Territorial Force on or prior to 30 September 1914, and to have served in an operational theatre outside the United Kingdom between 5 August 1914 and 11 November 1918. Those individuals who received either a 1914 Star or 1914/15 Star were not eligible for this award.

The Mercantile Marine War Medal, authorized in 1919, was awarded to those merchant seamen who undertook one or more voyages through areas of the sea specified as either a danger area or war zone. Although merchant seamen did not receive the Victory Medal it was actually possible for an individual to receive them both under certain circumstances. If an individual qualified for the Victory Medal first, left the Army and became a merchant seaman and then qualified for a Mercantile Marine War Medal, or vice versa. The medal roll for this award is separate from the War Office medal rolls for the First World War, and can be found under the reference BT 351. The roll is arranged in alphabetical order and is available on microfiche in the National Archives Open Reading Room.

The Silver War Badge (SWB), sometimes erroneously called the Silver Wound Badge, was authorized in September 1916 and takes the form of a circular silver badge with the legend 'For King and Empire — Services Rendered' surrounding the George V cipher. The badge was awarded to all of those military personnel who were discharged as a result of sickness or wounds contracted or received during the war, either at home or overseas. The badges are numbered on the back.

The medal rolls for all of these awards, apart from the Mercantile Marine War Medal, can be found in the record series WO 329. In order to access these rolls it is necessary to use the medal index cards, which are in the record series WO 372 and which are available on microfiche in the National Archives Open Reading Room.

9.2   Medal Index Cards

The medal index cards (MIC) in the record series WO 372 comprise over 10,000 sheets of microfiche, each containing 360 separate index cards. These cards were created by the Army Medal Office and consist of a name index in alphabetical order with the names then placed in 'Regimental Order of Precedence' (see Appendix 1). This means, for example, that if there were 200 John Smiths, they would be in a specific order that would be understood by the Army, rather than in random order. There are two collections of these cards: one for men and one for women. Both collections include officers and other ranks, as well as civilians.

The name order in the index cards usually conforms to the following sequence:

Jones J.
Jones James
Jones John
Jones Jonathan
Jones Julius
Jones J.A.
Jones J.A.A.
Jones J.B.A.
Jones J.C.

Each sheet of microfiche is arranged with the first of the 360 cards starting in the top left-hand corner, and the last card being in the bottom right-hand corner:

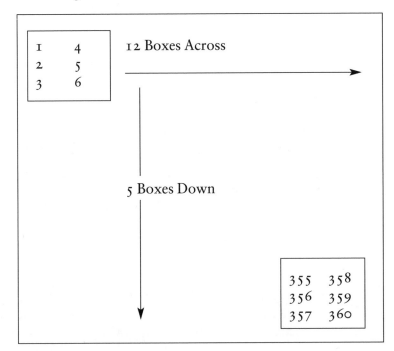

From this plan it can be seen that the first individual card is in the top left-hand corner, with the next two cards below that and the next three parallel to the first three. The MICs were filmed in boxes of six, with 12 blocks across and 5 blocks down.

The original medal index cards were produced in a number of varieties. An example of a typical card can be seen in Fig. 31. On many cards can be seen the word 'over'. On the back of about 10 per cent of the cards (mostly those for officers) was written correspondence information. This data has not been filmed by the National Archives, but is available via the Ancestry website *www.ancestry.co.uk*.

Each medal index card includes surname, initial(s) or forename(s), rank(s), number(s), regiment(s) or corps served in, the medals to which a man or woman was entitled (specifying each medal, the roll it is recorded on and the page of the roll), the first operational theatre served in, the date of entry to that theatre, and any important remarks.

An additional collection of medal index cards for the Indian Army, mostly for men of European or Anglo-Asian descent, can also be found on DocumentsOnline. These Indian Army medal index cards have been given the following references:

WO 372/25	Surnames A–E
WO 372/26	Surnames F–J
WO 372/27	Surnames K–O
WO 372/28	Surnames P–T
WO 372/29	Surnames U–Z

Apart from the medal roll references, the unit data and the date when an individual went overseas, information found in the remarks section of the medal index card can show if an individual was a prisoner of war, died of wounds or was killed in action, whether the

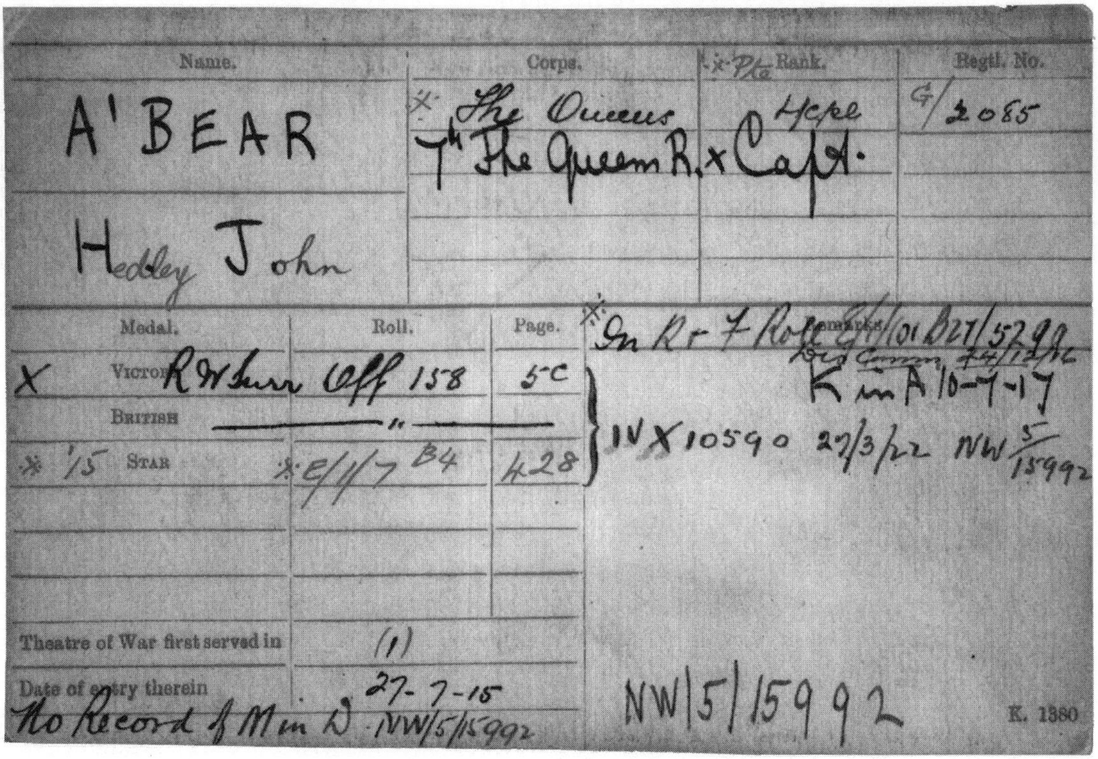
Name. Corps. Rank. Regtl. No.
A'BEAR
Hedley John
7th The Queen R. Capt.
Medal. Roll. Page. Remarks.
Victory
British
Star
Theatre of War first served in (1)
Date of entry therein 27-7-15
NW/5/15992
K. 1380

Fig. 31 *The Medal Index Card for Captain Hedley John A'Bear, recording not only his medal entitlement but also the fact that he was commissioned from the ranks and that he was killed in action.* WO 372

Fig. 32 (facing)
*The 1914/15 Star
medal rolls for the
Queen's Royal West
Surrey Regiment,
recording H.J.
A'Bear's entitlement
to the medal and the
date he went to
France.* WO 329/2614

individual was commissioned or if they transferred to the Royal Navy or Royal Air Force.

Below the list of medals for which an individual qualified there may be found the term 'Clasp and Roses', which indicates that the recipient of a 1914 Star also qualified for the dated bar for their medal because they had actually seen action under fire between 5 August and 22 November 1914.

An MIC may also include information about a number of other campaign medals awarded for service in Africa, India or the Middle East. Apart from the medal rolls for the Africa General Service Medal, which can be found in WO 100, the National Archives does not hold the medal rolls for post-war service in India or the Middle East.

Another medal that may be noted on the MIC is the award of the Territorial Force Efficiency Medal or Territorial Efficiency Medal to members of the Territorial Force. The National Archives does not hold a roll for these awards.

At the bottom of an MIC may be found the term 'EMB' or 'Emblems' and an alphanumeric reference, which indicates that the recipient of the medals was 'Mentioned in Despatches'. See 10.12 for further information.

9.2.1   *The Digitized Medal Index Cards*

The medal index cards (WO 372) have been digitized twice, once by the National Archives and once by Ancestry. The cards digitized by the National Archives do not include the backs of the cards, but they do include the Military Medal index cards and the campaign medal index for women. The Ancestry Medal index cards have had the backs digitized, but their collection lacks the MMs and the index for women.

To search the medal index cards at the National Archives you need to go to the DocumentsOnline section of the National Archives website.

It is possible to search for an MIC by surname and first name(s) and/or initial(s), rank, regiment or corps, and by number. Once you have located a card it is possible to download it (for a fee if outside the Archives) and print it.

In order to obtain the original medal roll, it is necessary to convert the Army Medal Office references found in the 'Roll' column and 'Page' column of the medal index card into a WO 329 document reference as explained in 9.4.

The Army Medal Office references not only provide the location of each medal roll — it is actually possible to interpret them to show which regimental/corps record office created the initial roll and also administered the unit's records of service.

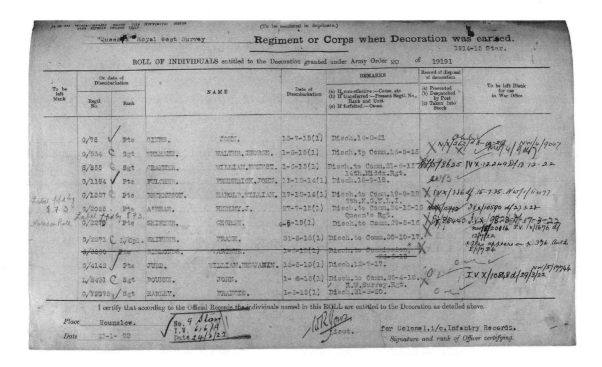

9.3 Medal Rolls

The medal rolls to which the medal index cards (WO 372) are the key can be found as original records under the reference WO 329. These medal rolls are split into a number of different rolls as follows:

British War and Victory Medals
1914 Star
1914/15 Star
Territorial Force War Medal
Silver War Badge

In most cases the rolls will tell which specific unit the individual served in to qualify for the medals. This is especially so regarding the 1914 and 1914/15 Star medal rolls. The rolls of the Silver War Badge will tell you when an individual joined the Army, when they were discharged and why, whether it was sickness or wounds. The SWB roll will also tell the ages of individuals on discharge and whether or not they served overseas.

9.4 How to Use the Medal Records

The medal index cards are the key to locating the correct medal roll(s) in WO 329. Once you have located the correct medal index card for an individual, it is necessary to consult two books before you are ready to order the medal rolls on the computer. The 'Key to the Medal Roll Index' will enable you to find the correct roll in WO 329/1. The 'Key' lists by medal where in WO 329/1 you need to look. Arranged by medal type and by other rank or officer, the 'Key' lists all of the different alphanumeric references and tells you on which page of WO 329/1 they can be found.

ARRANGEMENT OF 'THE KEY TO THE MEDAL ROLL INDEX'

Medal	Page
BWM and VM O/Rs	1–6
BWM and VM Off	7–13
1914 Star O/Rs	13–15
1914 Star Off	15–21
1914/15 Star O/Rs	21–4
1914/15 Star Off	24–30
TFWM O/Rs	30–3
TFWM Off	33–6
SWB All Ranks	37–9

Once you have located the relevant page, you need to see which page of the medal roll can be found in which WO 329 reference. Many of the medal rolls run to several thousands of pages. The correct WO 329 reference for a given medal roll is given on the right-hand side of the page in WO 329/1.

9.4.1   *Using H.J. A'Bear as an example*
Taking the 1914/15 Star which was qualified for first, the entry under the Roll column on the MIC states 'E/1/7b4', with the page number 428. Using the 'Key to the Medal Roll Index', the 1914/15 Star medal roll with this reference is on page 238 of WO 329/1. Page 428 of the medal roll with the original reference 'E/1/7b4' can be found in WO 329/2614. The page showing H.J. A'Bear can be seen in Fig. 32. H.J. A'Bear was commissioned in 1917. The medal roll entry for his British War Medal and Victory Medal are on Officer's Roll 158 page 5c. This roll entry is on page 10 of the 'Key' and notes that the correct reference for the medal roll is WO 329/2182.

The system of using the 'Key' and then WO 329 should help you to avoid ordering the wrong medal roll. When using the 'Key' make sure you use the correct medal section and the officer's or other rank's section as applicable.

9.5 Operational Theatres of War 1914–20: Alphanumeric Codes

The alphanumeric codes for each theatre of war, e.g. 1a relating to France and Belgium, are also used in the records of service. For those personnel who first saw operational service before 31 December 1915—and who therefore received either a 1914 Star or 1914/15 Star, as well as the British War and Victory Medals—the codes used differ slightly from those used for personnel who only saw their first operational service from 1 January 1916 onwards.

To 31/12/1915	From 1/1/1916
1	1 Western Europe
	a France and Belgium
	b Italy
2	2 Balkans
	a Greek Macedonia, Serbia, Bulgaria and European Turkey
	b Gallipoli (Dardanelles)
	3 Russia (4/5 August 1914–1/2 July 1920)
3	4 Egypt
	a 4/5 November 1914–18/19 March 1916
	b 18/19 March 1916–31 October/1 November 1918
4	5 Africa
	a East Africa, Nyasaland and Northern Rhodesia
	b South West Africa
	c Cameroon
	d Nigeria
	e Togoland
5	6 Asia
	a Hedjaz
	b Mesopotamia
	c Persia
	d Trans Caspia
	e South West Arabia
	f Aden
	g Frontier regions of India
	h Tsingtau
6	7 Australasia
	a New Britain

      b   New Ireland

      c   Kaiser Wilhelmland

      d   Admiralty Islands

      e   Nauru

      f   German Samoa

9.6 Regimental Order of Precedence

The regimental order of precedence is based on the date specific units were originally founded. The number at the end of each infantry regiment, starting with the Royal Scots, is the original numerical identity of the unit prior to 1881. It is the number used to identify the regiment in the officers index in WO 338, to denote which regiment an officer was first commissioned into. See 2.2 for further details.

The regimental order of precedence can be found in Appendix 1.

10 AWARDS FOR GALLANTRY AND MERITORIOUS SERVICE

Over 300,000 awards for gallantry or meritorious service were bestowed upon men and women of the British armed forces during the First World War. From the Victoria Cross to a Mentioned in Despatches, it is possible to find at least the date when the award was announced in the *London Gazette*. In many cases it is possible to find out exactly what an individual did to win an award, and in some cases, even when and where the deed was performed.

A number of awards were granted to non-British nationals, i.e. those who were not members of the British Empire. Such awards were not announced in the *London Gazette* but in numerous cases it is possible to find some mention of them amongst the records of the Foreign Office and War Office.

Many awards announced in the *London Gazette* were accompanied by a citation. The citation was the brief note that described the deed for which the award being announced was won. In many cases the citation was published some time after the award was announced in the *London Gazette*. For further information about this and other aspects of the *London Gazette* see 10.4.

Information concerning the institution of gallantry awards can be found in WO 32 Codes 50–2 and in *British Gallantry Awards* by P.E. Abbott and J.M.A. Tamplin.

10.1 The Process

The process by which an individual was recommended for an award needs to be understood, simply because the various parts of the process can provide the researcher with the opportunity to find out what the individual did to receive an award. From the actual recommendation for an award to the announcement of the award locally (in the operational theatre), the national announcement in the *London Gazette* to the receipt of the actual insignia, all could be recorded and the information preserved in archives.

The basic process was as follows:

Deed
Recommendation
Local Promulgation
National Promulgation
Receipt of Insignia

The deed was the act performed by an individual that was deemed to merit recognition.

The recommendation was the official paperwork submitted by the superior (usually commanding) officer of the person who performed the deed. The recommendation was usually submitted on an Army Form W 3121.

Local promulgation was where the award was announced in the various routine orders at army, corps, division or brigade level. Army Orders in this case are not to be confused with Army Orders for the whole British Army. Army Orders in this context are 1st, 2nd, 3rd, 4th or 5th Army Routine Orders.

National promulgation was where the award was announced in the *London Gazette*.

Receipt of insignia took two forms, either an investiture where the award was presented to the recipient or in the case of many Military Medals, for example, the award was sent by post to the recipient or their next of kin if they had died. A letter sent with most Military Medals stated that the award could have been presented in public, but many recipients had either died or chose not to receive their award in public.

10.2   Recommendations

Recommendations for awards were submitted on an Army Form W 3121, the vast majority of which were destroyed in the fire at the War Office records repository in Arnside Street in London on 8 September 1940. Some recommendations for awards may be found among the files in WO 158 concerning operations in East Africa. One file concerning recommendations for awards to members of the WAAC for the period December 1918 to December 1919 can be found in WO 165/65.

Access to recommendations for awards to Australian Imperial Force personnel can be made via the Australian War Memorial website *www.awm.gov.au*. For further information see chapter 14.3.

10.3 Citations

A citation is the brief description of the deed for which an award was granted, and it usually accompanies the announcement of the award when published in the *London Gazette*. In many cases the citation was published later than the announcement. In most cases it is possible to find the publication of the citation by consulting the index of the *London Gazette*. See 10.4 for further information.

No citations were published for awards announced in the New Year and Birthday Honours lists. Also, apart from those for a number

```
                 R O U T I N E   O R D E R S
                    XIII    C O R P S.
            ***********************************

                                      Sunday, 9th July, 1916.

              ADJUTANT GENERAL'S BRANCH.
              ===================

 318.    AWARDS.

              The Corps Commander has been pleased to award the
         Military Medal to the following N.C.O. and Men for acts
         of bravery:-

              No. 6944, Sergeant R.SEARLE, 11th Bn.,
                        Royal Fusiliers.

              No. 3992, Pte. A. STEWART, 11th Bn.,
                        Royal Scots.

              No.22675, Pte. W. EASTON,  11th Bn.,
                        Royal Scots.

 319.    TOWN MAJOR.

              Lieut. E.S.CUTTS, A.S.C., 30th Divisional Train,
         has been appointed TOWN MAJOR of SAILLY LAURETTE.
         Allotment of billets or bivouacs in SAILLY LAURETTE will
         be made by this Officer, and all questions regarding
         accommodation will be referred to him.

              QUARTERMASTER GENERAL'S BRANCH.
              =====================

                          N I L.

                     P.G.TWINING, Brigadier-General,

                     D. A. & Q. M. G., XIII CORPS.

                       N O T I C E.
                       =========

 LOST.  Between the hours of 10 p.m., 29th June and 6 a.m.
 30th June, a TRIUMPH Motor Bicycle No. 1022.B.   Was
 removed from a small trench off the BRONFAY ROAD, 100
 yards from its junction with PERONNE AVENUE.
         Any information regarding same to be sent to O.C.,
 30th Divisional Signal Company.
```

Fig. 33 *XIII Corps Routine Orders announcing a number of Military Medals, almost certainly for service on the Somme.* WO 95/898

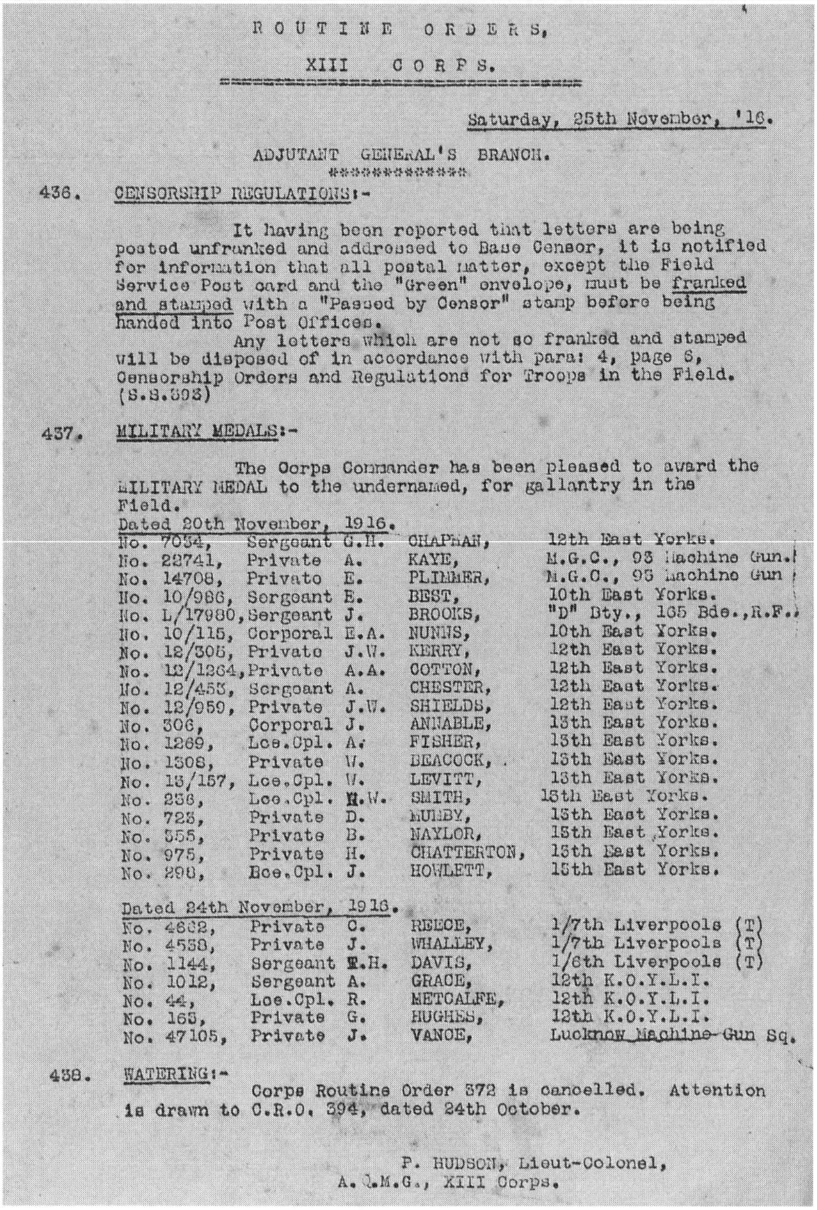

Fig. 34 *XIII Corps Routine Orders announcing a number of Military Medals; the date in the order is not the date upon which the award was won. These medals would have been announced in the* London Gazette *on various dates after this Routine Order.* WO 95/898

ROUTINE ORDERS,

XIII CORPS.

Saturday, 25th November, '16.

ADJUTANT GENERAL'S BRANCH.

436. CENSORSHIP REGULATIONS:-

It having been reported that letters are being posted unfranked and addressed to Base Censor, it is notified for information that all postal matter, except the Field Service Post card and the "Green" envelope, must be <u>franked</u> and stamped with a "Passed by Censor" stamp before being handed into Post Offices.

Any letters which are not so franked and stamped will be disposed of in accordance with para: 4, page 8, Censorship Orders and Regulations for Troops in the Field. (S.S.393)

437. MILITARY MEDALS:-

The Corps Commander has been pleased to award the MILITARY MEDAL to the undernamed, for gallantry in the Field.

Dated 20th November, 1916.

No. 7054,	Sergeant G.H.	CHAPMAN,	12th East Yorks.
No. 22741,	Private A.	KAYE,	M.G.C., 93 Machine Gun.
No. 14708,	Private E.	PLIMMER,	M.G.C., 93 Machine Gun
No. 10/986,	Sergeant E.	BEST,	10th East Yorks.
No. L/17980,	Sergeant J.	BROOKS,	"D" Bty., 165 Bde.,R.F..
No. 10/115,	Corporal E.A.	NUNNS,	10th East Yorks.
No. 12/305,	Private J.W.	KERRY,	12th East Yorks.
No. 12/1264,	Private A.A.	COTTON,	12th East Yorks.
No. 12/455,	Sergeant A.	CHESTER,	12th East Yorks.
No. 12/959,	Private J.W.	SHIELDS,	12th East Yorks.
No. 306,	Corporal J.	ANNABLE,	13th East Yorks.
No. 1269,	Lce.Cpl. A.	FISHER,	13th East Yorks.
No. 1508,	Private W.	BEACOCK,	13th East Yorks.
No. 13/157,	Lce.Cpl. W.	LEVITT,	13th East Yorks.
No. 236,	Lce.Cpl. H.W.	SMITH,	13th East Yorks.
No. 723,	Private D.	MUMBY,	13th East Yorks.
No. 555,	Private B.	NAYLOR,	13th East Yorks.
No. 975,	Private H.	CHATTERTON,	13th East Yorks.
No. 298,	Bce.Cpl. J.	HOWLETT,	13th East Yorks.

Dated 24th November, 1916.

No. 4662,	Private C.	REECE,	1/7th Liverpools (T)
No. 4558,	Private J.	WHALLEY,	1/7th Liverpools (T)
No. 1144,	Sergeant W.H.	DAVIS,	1/6th Liverpools (T)
No. 1012,	Sergeant A.	GRACE,	12th K.O.Y.L.I.
No. 44,	Lce.Cpl. R.	METCALFE,	12th K.O.Y.L.I.
No. 163,	Private G.	HUGHES,	12th K.O.Y.L.I.
No. 47105,	Private J.	VANOE,	Lucknow Machine-Gun Sq.

438. WATERING:-

Corps Routine Order 372 is cancelled. Attention is drawn to C.R.O. 394, dated 24th October.

P. HUDSON, Lieut-Colonel,
A.Q.M.G., XIII Corps.

of Military Medals awarded to nurses, no citations were published for the majority of MMs announced between 1916 and 1919.

10.4 The *London Gazette*

The *London Gazette* is an official newspaper of the state and has been in existence since 1665. Information found in the *London Gazette* includes commissions and announcements concerning honours and awards. The *London Gazette* is preserved in the National Archives in the record series ZJ 1. The indexes for the period 1914–20 are available on the open shelves in the Open Reading Room. All of the *London Gazettes* for the period 1914–20 are available on microfilm in the Open Reading Room.

To find an award in the *London Gazette* it is first necessary to consult the relevant *Gazette* index. Each index covers a three-month period, with that published in March also covering January and February, the June edition also covering April and May, the September edition also covering announcements made in July and August, and the December edition taking in October and November. The arrangement of each index is similar: in alphabetical order by the name of the award and then in alphabetical order by name of recipient. Alongside each name is a page number of a *London Gazette* published with the quarter of the year the index covers. Make a note of the page number, the number of the index (i.e. which quarter it covers) and the year, and take the information to the ZJ 1 catalogue.

During the First World War period, each month of the *London Gazette* had a different number of pages, many running into the thousands. The first page of the first *London Gazette* in January of any year is always page 1. The last page of the last *London Gazette* of December in the same year may be over page 12,000. By matching the page number of the entry to the relevant *Gazette*, already knowing that it can have only come from one of three months, you should find the relevant entry quite easily.

There are a number of indexes and finding aids that can help you to locate the award you seek and they are listed under the relevant awards.

On the card indexes of the DCM, MM and MSM, the date when the award was announced in the *London Gazette* is sometimes given as a number. These numbers and the corresponding dates are listed below:

Gazette No.	Date(s)
58	11 February 1919
59	11 February or 13 March 1919
60	18 or 24 or 30 January or 22 February 1919
61	29 March 1919
62	14 May 1919
63	17 June 1919
64	3 July 1919

65	23 July 1919
66	20 August 1919
67	20 August 1919
68	22 September 1919
69	16 October 1919
70	18 December 1919
Peace Gazette	3 June 1919
POW Gazette	30 January 1920

10.5 Colonial and Dominion Gazettes

Although the majority of awards granted during the First World War were announced in the *London Gazette*, awards given to troops of the Indian Army and the Australian Imperial Force, Canadian Expeditionary Force, New Zealand Expeditionary Force and South African Forces were also announced in their own gazettes. Many of these other gazettes are preserved at the National Archives.

A full list of Colonial and Dominion gazettes can be found on pages 104–9 of *Medals: the Researcher's Guide* (TNA, 2008). However, the following short list may help:

Australia Gazette	CO 559
Canada Gazette	CO 46
Gazette of India	V11/1–359 (at the British Library only)
New Zealand Gazette	CO 212
South Africa Gazette	CO 548

10.6 The Victoria Cross

The Victoria Cross (VC) is the supreme award for gallantry in the face of the enemy and as such was instituted in 1856. Some 633 Victoria Crosses were awarded during the First World War, this figure including two bars for second awards to Arthur Martin-Leake and Noel Chavasse. All awards of the VC are announced in the *London Gazette* and are accompanied by citations.

Recommendations for the award of the VC were submitted on an Army Form W 3121 and they had to be accompanied by at least three independent eyewitness statements. Once the recommendation paperwork had been passed up the chain of command, the final submission had to be passed to the Secretary of State for War and finally the King. The only complete submission that has survived (the remainder being destroyed in the Arnside Street fire on 8 September 1940) is that for Pte H. Christian, 2nd Battalion, King's Own Royal

Fig. 35 (facing) Military Cross Gazette Book *giving additional information such as the date and place the award was won. This additional information was not published in the* London Gazette. WO 389/2

Cross.

enemy, his party withdrew, and Capt. Price was the last man to leave. He had previously done fine work in the trenches during heavy bombardments. *La Bassee 2/6 June 1916.*

- Capt. William Hunter Riddell, M.B., Ind. Med. Serv.

For conspicuous gallantry and devotion to duty on several occasions when tending the wounded under heavy fire. *Lo clinn 8.3.16. Sannaiyat. 6+7 april 16* MESOPOTAMIA. *0137/2854 0137/2746*

- Temp. Capt. Thomas Rollason, 17th Bn., Midd'x R. *0137/2680.*

For conspicuous gallantry. He organised and carried out the seizure and consolidation of two newly-blown craters, and, when his two officers had become casualties, rallied his men and continued work under heavy fire. *Carency 2/6/16*

- Capt. Richard Arthur Stewart, M.B., R.A.M.C., Spec. Res. (attd. 2nd Bn., Border R.). *0137/2745.*

For conspicuous gallantry. During the attack on an enemy position he went forward and established an Aid Post in a mine crater, and tended many wounded under heavy shell fire. His coolness and disregard of personal safety gave great confidence to those round him. *Mametz 1.7.16.*

- Capt. George Willard Treleaven, Can. Army Med. Corps. *0137/2706.*

For conspicuous gallantry and devotion to duty when attending wounded men under heavy shell fire, and getting them into safety. *Dickebusch 5.6.16.*

- Capt. Edward William Wales, Line. R. (attd. 2/5th Bn., Glouc. R., T.F.). *0137/2713*

For conspicuous gallantry. He led a raid with great dash through heavy machine-gun and shrapnel fire from a flank. He personally threw two bombs into an enemy machine-gun emplacement, and silenced the gun. He was wounded. *Fauquissart — 20/21 June 1916.*

- Lt. Alexander William Aitchison, 13th Can. Infy. Bn. *0137/2735*

For conspicuous gallantry in leading forward a party of bombers and rifles through the enemy's barrage in order to occupy an important point. His gallant act removed a great danger. *The Crater 19/4/16. Bluff.*

- Lt. James Creswell Auld, 16th By., Canadian Fld. Arty. *0137/2651.*

For conspicuous gallantry. When his Observation Post was hit by a shell, which wounded him severely and his telephonist mortally, he endeavoured to rescue the latter from the *debris*. Being unable to do so, he went 300 yards under heavy fire for assistance. He then returned and helped to carry his telephonist to a place of safety. *St. Eloi. 1.5.16.*

- Temp. Lt. Richard Nunn Aylward, 204th Fd. Co., R.E. *0137/2706.*

For conspicuous gallantry. When a raiding party had withdrawn from the enemy's trench he led a small R.E. party into the trench and blew up a machine-gun emplacement. He has frequently shown great courage and determination when reconnoitring. *Neuve Chapelle 8.6.16.*

- Lt. (temp. Capt.) Rainsford Balcombe-Brown, R.F.A., Spec. Res., and R.F.C. *0137/2713*

For conspicuous gallantry and skill. He attacked an enemy kite balloon and brought it down in flames. He was flying in a type of machine unfamiliar to him owing to the absence through wounds of the regular pilot. At dawn he commenced to learn the machine, and the same evening brought down the kite. *Guns 26th 1916.*

- Lt. (temp. Capt.) Samuel Boyle, 1/4th Bn., R. Berks. R., T.F. *0137/2651*

For conspicuous gallantry. After a heavy bombardment the enemy raided his trench. Captain Boyle displayed great energy and courage, shot the leading enemy as he appeared on the parapet, organised bombing parties, dug out buried men, cleared the trench of the enemy, and handled the situation generally in a masterly manner. *Hebuterne 15/16 May 1916.*

- Temp. Lt. Rawdon Briggs, 75th Field Co., R.E. *0137/2657*

For conspicuous gallantry under heavy fire. Lt. Briggs assisted in carrying a wounded officer to the dressing station, and later, under heavy fire, succeeded with his section in removing an obstruction from a road. *St Jean 6/7th May 1916.*

- Temp. Lt. John Gordon Brown, General List (attd. Y/47th Trench Mortar Bty.). *0137/2745*

For conspicuous gallantry. He continued to work his guns under very heavy hostile shell fire, and silenced the enemy's guns after three hours of fighting. On another occasion his battery was engaged during three successive days, and, when his guns were buried and dug-outs blown in, he kept up fire with one gun while the others were being dug out. He has set a fine example to his men. *Souchez Section. 19.6.16.*

- Lt. Peter Louis Stuart Browne, 22nd Canadian Infy. Bn. *0137/2657.*

For conspicuous gallantry. He was holding a portion of the front line trench with a machine-gun and six men, when the enemy, after a heavy bombardment, attacked. He worked his gun till it was put out of action, and then, picking up a few more men, bayonetted his way through the enemy, killing several. Finally he checked any further advance by the enemy, till he was relieved. *St. Eloi. 4/5 April 1916.*

- Lt. (temp. Capt.) Harvey Bruce Buckley, R.A., Spec. Res. *0137/2683*

For conspicuous gallantry and good service, notably when cutting wire with his guns previous to raids on the enemy's trenches. He has also done fine work under heavy fire as observing officer in the front line trenches. *12th + 13th June 1916. Ypres.*

- Temp. Lt. William Walter Busby, 13th Bn., Essex R. *0137/2738*

For conspicuous gallantry during a successful raid. He led his men with great dash into the enemy's trenches, and, after the withdrawal, remained for some time assisting to find and bring in the wounded. *Souchez, 1/2 July 1916.*

- Lt. (temp. Capt.) Edward Christian, "B" Bty., 5th Lond. Bde., R.F.A., T.F. (attd. C/235th Bty.). *0137/2671*

For gallantry and devotion to duty. After the wires to his observing station had been cut he laid a wire to an unprotected and exposed spot under heavy shell fire.

Lancaster Regiment, which can be found in WO 32/21402.

The registers of the VC can be found in WO 98. This register contains, in *Gazette* date order, the citations and in many cases the date of death of all winners of the VC from the First World War. WO 98/5 contains a list of all VCs by division and unit. WO 98/6 is an alphabetical list of Victoria Crosses awarded from 1914 to 1920. The register for 1900–44 is in WO 98/8.

The registers of the VC have been digitized and placed on DocumentsOnline, where it is possible to search for VC recipients by name.

10.7   The Distinguished Service Order

The Distinguished Service Order (DSO) was instituted in 1886 as a reward for meritorious or distinguished service. The award was initially for those officers not eligible for the CB (Companion of the Most Honourable Order of the Bath), but during the First World War the award was bestowed upon officers from the rank of 2nd lieutenant to brigadier general. Once the Military Cross was instituted in 1914 (see 10.8), it was unusual for officers below lieutenant and even captain to be awarded the DSO.

Announcement of awards of the DSO can be found in the *London Gazette* (see 10.4). Awards announced as part of the New Year or Birthday Honours lists were primarily for meritorious service and not for gallantry in action, and as such these awards are not accompanied by a citation.

The register of the DSO can be found in WO 390 and is arranged by the date when the award was announced in the *London Gazette*. The entries in WO 390 provide the citation, the date when the award was presented to the recipient or when it was sent by post, and in some cases the date when the recipient died (even after the war). WO 390 is available on microfilm.

The DSO and MC Gazette Book in WO 389 contains copies of the *London Gazette,* which were given to the War Office just prior to publication. These advance copies are arranged in chronological order and then by DSO and MC, and are then annotated in most cases with the place and date of the deed for which the award was being granted. The date and place can be used with information found in the war diaries in WO 95 (see 7.2).

The DSO and MC Gazette Books can be found in WO 389/1–8 and are available on microfilm.

Apart from using the *London Gazette* to find out when an award was gazetted, it is possible to find the date when the award was announced, and in some cases other biographical data, by consulting *The Distinguished Service Order* by General Sir O'Moore Creagh and Miss E.M. Humphris, a copy of which is available in the National Archives Library.

10.8   The Military Cross

The Military Cross (MC) was instituted in late 1914 as a reward for gallantry or meritorious service performed by officers of the rank of captain and below, and warrant officers. As with other decorations for gallantry or meritorious service, all awards of the Military Cross are announced in the *London Gazette* (see 10.4).

Although information regarding the MC can be found in the *London Gazette* (which can be time consuming), there is a name index together with annotated copies of the *London Gazette* on microfilm in the record series WO 389. WO 389/1–8, called the Gazette Books, are copies of the *London Gazette* that were kept by the War Office and then in many cases annotated with the date and place of the action for which the MC was awarded. WO 389/9–24 is the name index, which will provide name, rank and unit of the MC recipient and the date when the award was announced in the *London Gazette*. By applying the *Gazette* date to WO 389/1–8, you should be able to find the citation for the award.

MCs announced as part of the New Year or Birthday Honours lists were for meritorious service rather than gallantry in action, and as such are not accompanied by a citation.

10.9   The Distinguished Conduct Medal

The Distinguished Conduct Medal (DCM) was instituted in 1854 as an award for all other ranks for distinguished service in the field. As with other awards, all awards of the DCM, apart from those to foreign nationals, are announced in the *London Gazette*. Most announcements are accompanied by a citation, but some awards announced in the New Year or Birthday Honours lists have no citations.

A nominal card index of DCM recipients, giving name, rank, number, unit and the date when the award was announced in the *London Gazette*, is available in the Open Reading Room.

The DCM nominal index has been digitized and placed on Documents-Online, where it is possible to search by name, number or unit. The National Archives reference for the DCM card index online is WO 372/23.

A published roll of the DCM can be found in *Recipients of the Distinguished Conduct Medal 1914–1920* by R.W. Walker. Once again, this book provides the same data as the card index. The book is available in the National Archives Library.

The citations for all First World War DCMs announced in the *London Gazette* have been collected together into a newly published work. Arranged by regiment or corps and then in alphabetical order, *Citations of the Distinguished Conduct Medal 1914–1920* by R.W. Walker and C. Buckland enables the researcher to cut a number of corners and go directly to the citation for an award. A copy of the DCM citations book is available in the library at the National Archives.

Although the citations will tell you what an individual did to earn their DCM, the citations do not always give the date of the deed or, in most cases, where the deed was performed. The DCM Gazette Books in WO 391, arranged by *Gazette* date, contain copies of citations for the DCM, and most are annotated with the specific date and place when and where the award was earned. WO 391 is available on microfilm in the Open Reading Room.

10.10   The Military Medal

The Military Medal (MM) was instituted in March 1916 and, apart from two very early awards, the first awards were announced in the *London Gazette* on 3 June 1916. The MM was created as an award for warrant officers, NCOs and men. The award was also available to women.

A nominal index of MM winners, giving name, rank, number, units and the *London Gazette* date, is available in the Open Reading Room. This index has been digitized and placed on DocumentsOnline and can be searched by name, number and unit. MM index cards on DocumentsOnline are given the National Archives reference WO 372/23.

10.11   The Meritorious Service Medal

Originally conceived as an award for long and meritorious service for other ranks (the recipient also being awarded an annuity), the warrant of the Meritorious Service Medal (MSM) was altered during the First World War due to the need for an award for service not in the face of the enemy. From 1916 the MSM was awarded for meritorious service or gallantry not in the face of the enemy; such MSMs

without an annuity. All awards of these non-annuity or
known as immediate MSMs, were announced in the
te. Unlike an annuity MSM, the naming on an imme-
udes the recipient's number.

d index in the Open Reading Room listing awards of
ard index provides name, rank, number, regiment or
rational theatre the award was won in, and the date
was announced in the *London Gazette*. The card
in alphabetical order.

index has been digitized and placed on Documents-
possible to search by name, number or unit. The
eference for the MSM card index is WO 372/24.

f all the immediate MSMs awarded between 1916
award was replaced by the British Empire Medal
d in *Meritorious Service Medal. The Immediate*
by Ian McInnes, a copy of which is available in
Library.

10   patches

ed in Despatches (MiD) was the lowest form
vice performed during the war that was
Gazette*. Originally only an award that was
e record of service), towards the end of the
some form of visible mark to show that an
n an MiD. After much discussion, the
ow an oakleaf emblem to be worn on the
dal. Only one oakleaf emblem could be
n individual was Mentioned in Despatches.
h time an individual was mentioned he
bearing his full service details, the date
and the date it was announced in the

se who were Mentioned in Despatches,
p   the *Gazette* date, is available in the
O   iD card index has also been digitized
an   ne, where it has been given the refer-
enc

10.13 The Royal Red Cross

Instituted in 1883 as a reward for nurses, the Royal Red Cross (RRC) was further expanded in 1915 by the addition of a second class award, the Associate of the Royal Red Cross (ARRC). Any nurses awarded an ARRC could be promoted within the award and awarded an RRC. In 1917 a bar was authorized for the RRC only. Any nurse who was already holding an ARRC and who was awarded the award again, was given an RRC.

All awards were announced in the *London Gazette*. The register of the Royal Red Cross (both classes) is in WO 145.

The register of the RRC in WO 145 is arranged as follows, the dates being the *Gazette* dates:

WO 145/1	1883–1918
WO 145/2	1918–43
WO 145/3	1943–94

These registers are indexed by name and each entry will provide the relevant page number.

10.14 Indian Army Awards

10.14.1 *Awards to Indian Army native soldiers*

During the First World War the majority of Indian Army native soldiers were given awards that were unique to the Indian Army. Although it was possible for native troops to receive the Victoria Cross (11 were so awarded; 6 for France, 3 for Mesopotamia and 2 for Egypt) and Indian Army native officers to receive the Military Cross, they were usually given one of the awards listed below.

The best secondary source to consult for information about awards given to Indian Army native soldiers is *Honours and Awards Indian Army 1914–1921*.

10.14.2 *Records of the India Office*

Although all awards for gallantry and meritorious service to members of the British and Indian Armies were announced in the *London Gazette*, one file, in the British Library, is worth consulting above all others. L/MIL/17/5/2416 contains a list of awards granted to Indian Officers (Native), NCOs and men and followers of the Indian Army and Imperial Service Troops (Indian State Forces) in all theatres during the First World War. Broken down by award from the VC down, this book provides full service details, where the award was earned and any salient remarks. The work also includes foreign awards, promotions and gratuities.

10.14.3 *The Order of British India*

Originally instituted in 1839, the Order of British India (OBI) was a reward for meritorious service and was awarded in two classes to Indian commissioned officers. As with other awards, the OBI was announced in the *Gazette of India*.

10.14.4 *The Indian Order of Merit*

The Indian Order of Merit (IOM) was instituted by the Honourable East India Company in 1837. During the First World War period the award was available in two classes and was awarded to native Indian soldiers. Awards of the IOM were announced in the *Gazette of India*.

10.14.5 *The Indian Distinguished Service Medal*

Instituted in 1907 as an award for Indian commissioned officers, non-commissioned officers and other ranks of the Indian Army, awards of the Indian Distinguished Service Medal (IDSM) were announced in the *Gazette of India*. A bar for subsequent awards was authorized in 1917 and the award was extended to those non-combatants serving in the field.

10.15 Orders of Chivalry

The award of any order of chivalry was announced in the *London Gazette*. The most common awards made prior to 1917 were to the Most Honourable Order of the Bath and the Most Distinguished Order of Saint Michael and Saint George. These awards were only open to officers. The Most Excellent Order of the British Empire, which was instituted in 1917, was open to warrant officers and above. *Burke's Handbook of the Order of the British Empire* of 1921 lists all appointments to the Order between 1917 and late 1920. A copy of this book is available in the National Archives Library.

Some information about appointments to the Order of the Bath can be found in WO 103.

10.16 Foreign Awards

Many men and women of the British Army were given awards by allied nations. Many foreign awards given to personnel of the British Army were announced in the *London Gazette*. However, a significant number of awards, especially those given to other ranks, were not announced in the *London Gazette* and finding information to verify entitlement to such awards can be very frustrating and in many cases fruitless.

There are two key series of records where information about foreign awards given to Britons can be found.

War Office records concerning foreign awards given to Britons can be found in WO 388. This series lists by the bestowing country and *London Gazette* date, the names of those individuals who received such awards as the Croix de Guerre and Légion d'Honneur. The records in WO 388 also list a number of awards that were not announced in the *London Gazette*, especially those given in the early months of the war. WO 388 is available on microfilm in the Open Reading Room.

The second key series of records where information about foreign awards given to British nationals may be found are the records of the Foreign Office Treaty Department in FO 372. This series is arranged by year and then in alphabetical order by country.

The Treaty Department was responsible for more than just awards, and identifying relevant files concerning awards requires skill. The best way to identify relevant files is to use the Foreign Office (FO) card index in the entrance to the Document Reading Room. Guidance about using the card index is available on or near the index.

There are two approaches to using the FO card index. The first approach means looking for the name of the recipient of a foreign award. The second approach is a search under the heading of 'Orders' and then the name of the bestowing country. In both cases any FO references found on a card require converting into an FO 372 document reference.

The amount of information you may find in an FO Treaty Department file can vary dramatically. You may find a detailed recommendation for the award (it may be in English or the language of the bestowing country) or you may just find a list of names and the award being given. If the award was not announced in the *London Gazette* and yet you find evidence of the award in FO 372, deciding if an individual was or was not entitled to the award is a matter that in most cases will not be easily resolved.

There are a number of other places where entitlement to Foreign Awards may be found. The first place to look would be in the unit war diaries in WO 95 and the second would be in any regimental or unit history.

11 COURTS MARTIAL

Thousands of men were tried by court martial for offences committed during the First World War. Depending upon the offence committed, the type of court martial where the accused was tried dictates whether any records survive concerning the case.

Over 3,000 men were sentenced to death as a result of a court martial, but the majority of these sentences were commuted to other punishments such as terms of imprisonment.

In accordance with paragraph 359 of the Armed Forces Act 2006, those men who were executed for military offences were pardoned. Sections 3a and 3b of paragraph 359 of the Act laid down the offences covered by the pardon and these were as follows:

OFFENCES UNDER PROVISIONS OF THE ARMY ACT 1881
Casting away arms
Cowardice
Quitting their post
Sleeping on sentry duty
Mutiny
Striking a superior officer
Disobedience
Desertion or attempting to desert

OFFENCES UNDER PROVISIONS OF THE INDIAN ARMY ACT 1911
Casting away arms and cowardice
Sleeping on sentry duty
Quitting their post
Mutiny and disobedience
Desertion or attempting to desert

The WO 71 Courts Martial proceedings for these men have been annotated to that effect. Apart from the registers of courts martial in WO 213, which lists all those tried by court martial, the only other major source is the proceedings of courts martial, primarily concering those where the accused was executed.

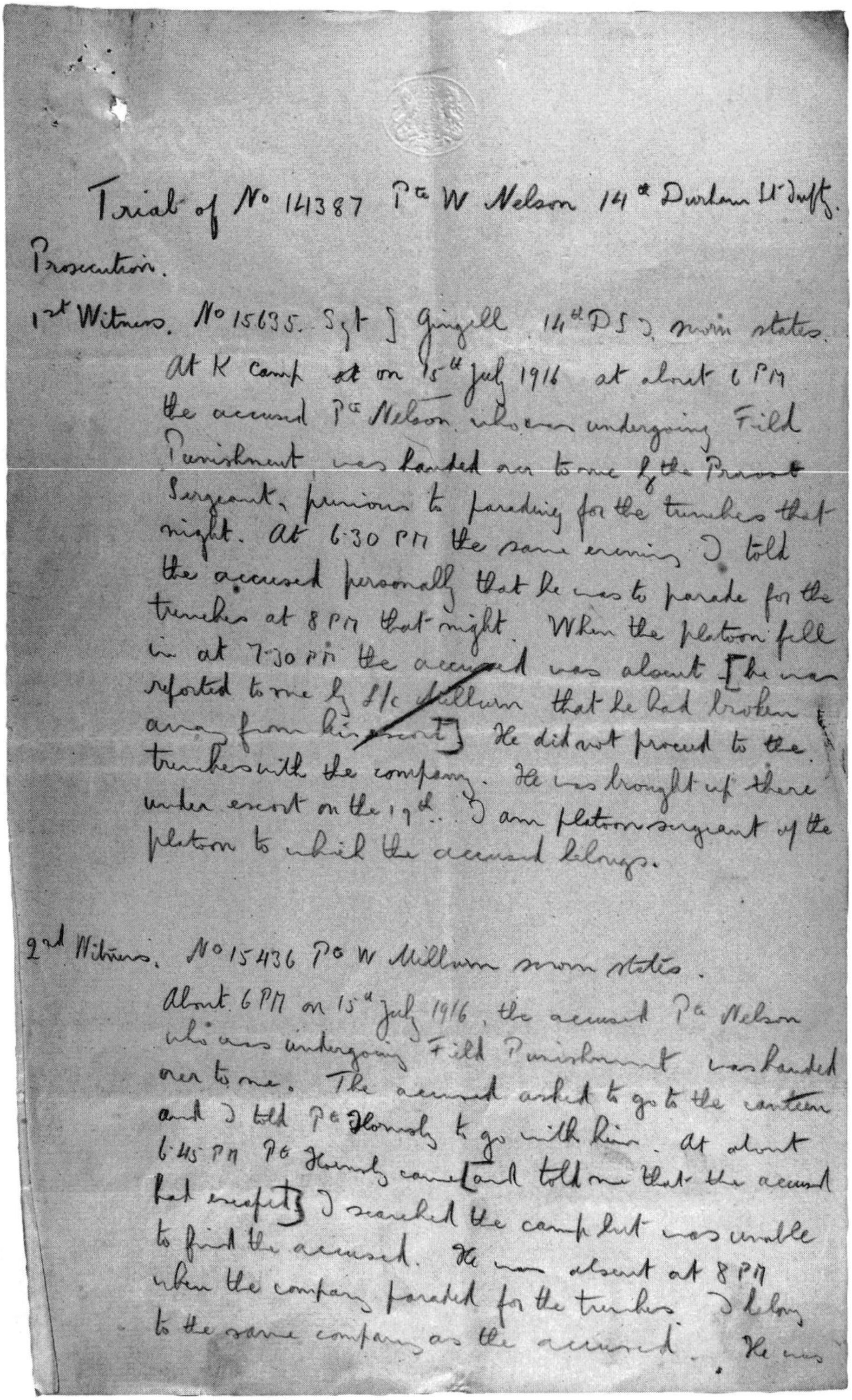

Trial of N° 14387 P.te W Nelson 14th Durham L.t Infty.

Prosecution.

1st Witness. N° 15635. Sgt J Gingell 14th DLI, sworn states.

At K camp at on 15th July 1916 at about 6 P.M the accused P.te Nelson who was undergoing Field Punishment was handed over to one of the Provost Sergeant, previous to parading for the trenches that night. At 6.30 P.M the same evening I told the accused personally that he was to parade for the trenches at 8 P.M that night. When the platoon fell in at 7.30 P.M the accused was absent [he was reported to me by L/c Milburn that he had broken away from his escort] He did not proceed to the trenches with the company. He was brought up there under escort on the 19th. I am platoon sergeant of the platoon to which the accused belongs.

2nd Witness. N° 15436 P.te W Milburn sworn states.

About 6 P.M on 15th July 1916, the accused P.te Nelson who was undergoing Field Punishment was handed over to me. The accused asked to go to the canteen and I told P.te Hornsby to go with him. At about 6.45 P.M P.te Hornsby came and told me that the accused had escaped. I searched the camp but was unable to find the accused. He was absent at 8 P.M when the company paraded for the trenches. I belong to the same company as the accused. He was

Fig. 36
Proceedings from
the Field General
Court Martial of
Private William
Nelson.
WO 71/488

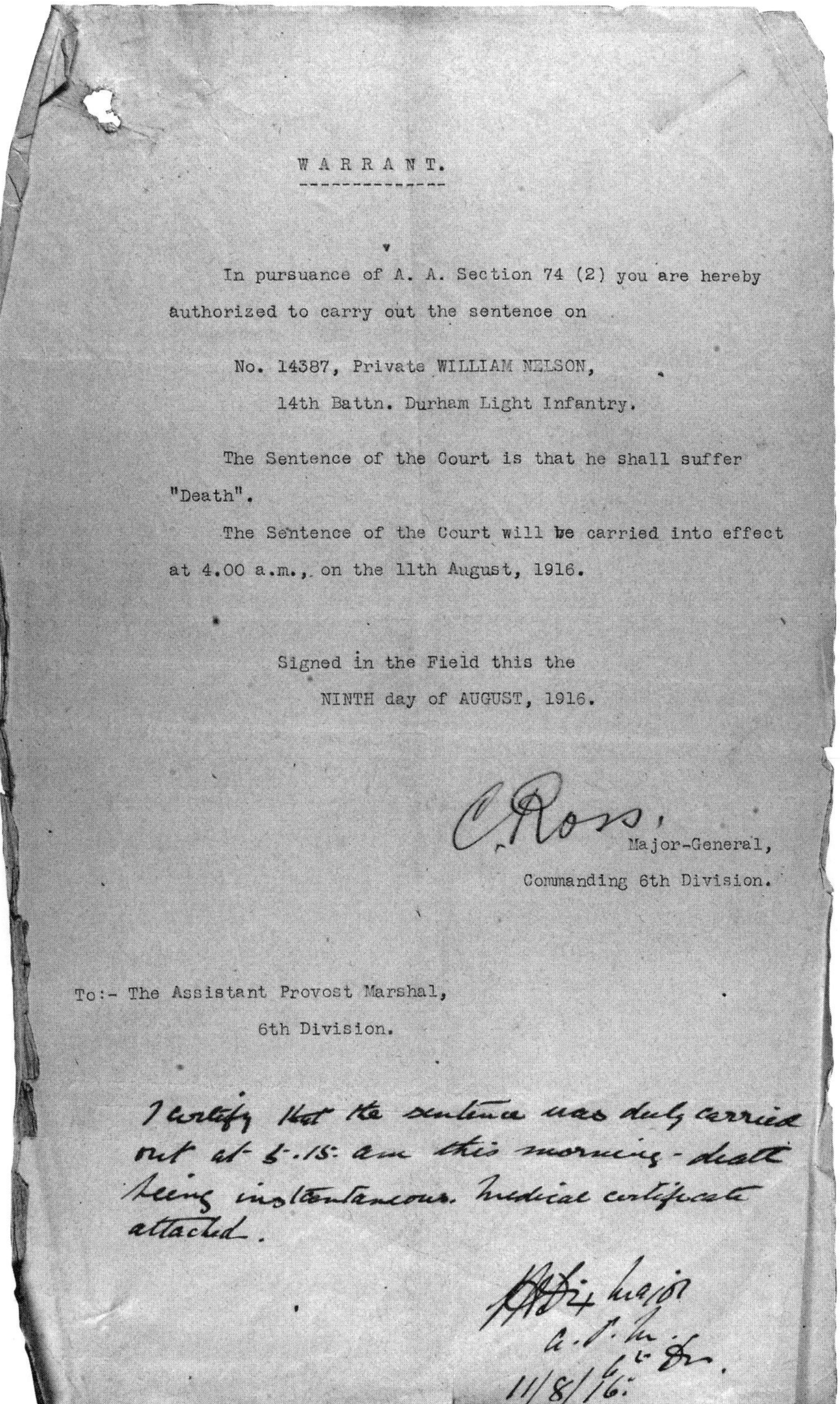

WARRANT.

In pursuance of A. A. Section 74 (2) you are hereby authorized to carry out the sentence on

No. 14387, Private WILLIAM NELSON,

14th Battn. Durham Light Infantry.

The Sentence of the Court is that he shall suffer "Death".

The Sentence of the Court will be carried into effect at 4.00 a.m., on the 11th August, 1916.

Signed in the Field this the

NINTH day of AUGUST, 1916.

C. Ross, Major-General,

Commanding 6th Division.

To:- The Assistant Provost Marshal,

6th Division.

I certify that the sentence was duly carried out at 5.15 am this morning – death being instantaneous. Medical certificate attached.

[illegible] Major

A.P.M.

6th Div.

11/8/16.

Fig. 37 *Death Warrant for the execution of Private William Nelson of 14 DLI. William Nelson was pardoned in 2006.* WO 71/488

When received	Appeal from Summary Award of C.O.	Rank		Name	Battalion	Regiment	Where Held	Date of Trial	Offence against Inhabitant
3		R.	W.	Burrell	2	R. Sussex.	Les Brebis	May 5	
		P.		Tarm		R.A.M.C.,	Le Tepot	. 5	
		Rf.	P.	Gribben	1	R. I. Rif.	bernancourt	April 20	
		.	P.	Kane	1	.	.	. 20	
		R.	W.	Cunningham		A. S. C,	Marseilles	May 1	

Fig. 38 *Judge Advocate General's Register of Courts Martial.* WO 213/9

Research Guide, Military Information Leaflet 22, 'Army: Courts Martial, 17th–20th Centuries' can provide some basic information.

11.1 Courts Martial Proceedings (WO 71)

The records preserved in the record series WO 71 consist of trial proceedings of those courts martial held to try the most serious military crimes. The majority of the files are for men executed for murder, desertion and other offences that carried the death penalty. Arranged in chronological order by date of trial, it is possible to search the online catalogue by name of the accused.

An example of a WO 71 record can be seen in Figs. 36 and 37. The subject of this example, Private William Nelson 14 DLI, is pictured on the cover of *Death Sentences* by Gerard Oram.

11.2 Registers of Courts Martial

Registers of Field General Courts Martial, containing the names of the accused, his rank, regiment or corps, place of trial, charge and sentence, can be found in WO 213/2–26. Registers of District Courts Martial containing similar information but for lesser offences can be found in WO 86/62–5. Registers of General Courts Martial that took place abroad are in WO 90/6–8.

If an individual was tried by court martial, the date and place where the trial took place, together with the charge(s) and, if found guilty, the sentence, should be annotated on the individual's AF B103 Casualty Form — Active Service. Details concerning courts martial may also be found on the Regimental, Company or Field Conduct Sheet, Army Form B 121 or B 122.

An example of a WO 213 register can be seen in Fig. 38.

						NATURE OF CHARGE														SENTENCE						
Cowardice	Desertion	Absence and Breaking out of Barracks (B) or Camp (C)	Striking or Violence to S.O.	Insubordination and Threatening	Disobedience	Quitting (Q) or Sleeping (S) on Post	Drunkenness	Injuring or Making away with Property &c.	Losing Property &c.	Theft	Indecency	Resisting or Escaping Escort	Escaping Confinement	Miscellaneous	Death	Penal Servitude	Imprisonment	Detention	Field Punishment	Discharge with Ignominy	Reduction in rank and Loss of Seniority	Stoppages Fines and Forfeiture of Pay	Not Guilty	Remitted	Remarks
	do													S.4o(4)	do									do		
do															do										S:com.
do															do										S. —
						do															3no2.d				

11.3   Other Courts Martial Records

The only other significant records concerning courts martial are the records kept in WO 93. Among these records are nominal rolls for Australians tried by court martial in WO 93/42, and Canadians tried by court martial in WO 93/43–5.

11.4   Published Sources

There are a number of very important books concerning courts martial, many of which provide information not only about the cases, but also about the accused. Copies of all the following can be found in the National Archives Library.

Gerard Oram's book *Death Sentences Passed by Military Courts of the British Army 1914–1920*, arranged alphabetically, lists those who were sentenced to death, even if the sentence was commuted, with rank, number, regiment and offence. This book also gives National Archives document references, mostly from WO 71 and WO 213.

Julian Putkowski's *British Army Mutineers 1914–1922* lists by name all those tried for mutiny and provides service details, National Archives document references and some contextual information about the mutinies.

The definitive work on those soldiers executed during the First World War is *Shot at Dawn* by Julian Putkowski and Julian Sykes. This book not only provides brief information about each case but also details further information regarding those executed and includes numerous National Archives document references.

A recent work concerning soldiers from Ireland who were executed during the First World War, and which brings the matter of executed soldiers right up to date, is *Forgotten Soldiers: The Irishmen Shot at Dawn* by Stephen Walker.

CONFIDENTIAL.   2.A.

Reference 119843/5   (A.G.3.)   (Dec. 31. 1918)   Dated, Jan. 2nd 1919

Name in full Malcolm Murray Lyon   Rank in time of Capture 2nd Lieut.

Date of Capture 26/11/16 Place of Capture. Beaumont-Hamel (near) Serre

If wounded or otherwise. Slight bayonet wound in left foot.

*Company etc. 'C'   Unit 16th (S) Batt. Highland L.I. 97th (I) Brigade. 32nd Division.

Whether Escaped or Repatriated. Repatriated   Date of Escape or Repatriation 21/11/18

Date of arrival in England. 29/11/18

Present address. 8 Sherwood Rise. Nottingham.

*(NOTE:—Refers to Unit etc., in which serving at time of capture).

STATEMENT regarding circumstances which led to capture :—

We attacked on the morning of Nov. 18. 1916, the purpose being to capture the German first and second lines.

I reached the second line with my platoon, but no forces came up on right or left, and the Germans regained possession of their front line. About mid-day of the same day we discovered we were surrounded & dug ourselves in. Throughout the day stragglers & wounded came into us & the wounded were put in the dug-out. Each night patrols went out, but reported that it was impossible to get through the German lines unless we left our wounded (now numbering 60). In view of this & the shortage of bombs &c, and the very slight chance of any of us getting through if we did try a rush ; we decided to hold on and wait relief.

Of the six officers, only three of us were able to do duty, & one of these (Lieut. Stewart. 16. H.L.I) was captured on the third night. The others, either being wounded or suffering from shell-shock had to remain in the dug-out.

The Germans attacked us each day but were driven off, largely owing to the devotion to duty of our Lewis gunners, all of whom were killed or wounded before the end. On the fifth day a Brigade attempted to relieve us but was unable to penetrate the German lines. Meanwhile our food & water supply had given out & it was difficult to keep the seriously wounded alive. The Germans continued to attack us — unsuccessfully — and we took about 15 prisoners

On the eighth afternoon (Nov. 26. 1916) the sentries were overcome before they could raise the alarm. the dug-out was bombed and we were taken prisoner.

X 11

To
The Secretary, War Office,
   Whitehall, London, S.W.1.

(1063) W7716/HP4609 24,000 11/18 Cax.P.Ltd. H1345

(signed)   Malcolm M. Lyon. Lieut.
3/att 16/ Highland Light Inf.

12 PRISONERS OF WAR

During the First World War 7335 officers and 174,491 men were captured by the enemy. Interestingly, about half of this number fell into German hands between 21 March and 11 November 1918 (from the start of the German spring offensive to the armistice). Many officers and men were also captured in other operational theatres.

Although there are numerous records concerning prisoners of war, the majority being Foreign Office correspondence concerning prison camps and the care of the men being held in them, the most informative records concerning capture and life as a prisoner are those found in wo 161. In the case of officers who were captured, it is also possible to find their repatriation reports.

12.1　WO 161

A small selection of prisoner of war debrief records can be found in wo 161/95–101. These records were created by the Committee on the Treatment of British Prisoners of War and contain interviews and reports. They are split into officers (wo 161/95–96), medical officers (wo 161/97) and other ranks (wo 161/98–100). The index to these papers is in wo 161/101. The index contains name, subject and place indexes. A copy of this index is on the open shelves of printed National Archives catalogues near the staff desk in the Open Reading Room. Many of the references in the index refer to reports that were never printed and are consequently no longer available.

The best way to locate reports in wo 161 is by computer. wo 161 has been digitized and paced on DocumentsOnline where it is possible to search by the name of the prisoner or war, his regiment or corps or the place where they were held. If you obtain any results for your search, it is possible to download and print off copies of the report. If you are accessing DocumentsOnline from outside the National Archives, you will have to pay a fee to download the report.

Another index of wo 161 is available in the 'Behind the Wire'

Fig. 39 *A repatriation report completed by an officer after he had been repatriated as a prisoner of war.*
WO 339/49656

section of the First World War website *www.1914–1918.net* but it does not provide access to the reports, nor does it advise which reports mentioned in the index were not printed and are therefore not available.

12.2 Repatriation Reports

All those officers who were captured and who returned home after the war had to complete a report into the circumstances of their capture. The main purpose of these reports was to ascertain the conduct of the officer and to ensure that he had not surrendered in suspicious circumstances.

On the medal index cards of many officers can be found the term 'Exonerated Officers List'. This was a list of officers who had been prisoners of war and, after their repatriation report had been considered and accepted by the committee set up to examine them, were then permitted to be awarded their campaign medals. This list no longer exists.

An example of a repatriation report can be seen in Fig. 39.

12.3 Other Sources

A printed list of officers who became prisoners of war can be found in *List of Officers taken prisoner in the Various Theatres of War between August 1914 and November 1918*, compiled by the military agents Cox and Co. A copy of this book can be found in the National Archives Library.

A number of lists of prisoners of war can be found amongst the ADM and AIR record series, but they are not at all comprehensive. Correspondence concerning prisoners of war can be found in FO 383 Foreign Office: Prisoners of War and Aliens Department: General Correspondence from 1915–1919, which, while not containing full lists, is liberally scattered with names. This series can be accessed by using the FO card index and the registers in FO 566 and FO 662.

However, FO 383 has been extensively catalogued and it is now possible to do keyword searches on the Catalogue to find mention of individuals such as prisoners or internees, or places where people were held as prisoners or internees.

13 CASUALTIES AND WAR DEAD

During the First World War the British Empire suffered over two million casualties, and nearly one million men and women were either killed or died. Specific records concerning the dead are very inconsistent in the information they provide. It is frequently the case that no records can be found. If no information is found in the unit war diary (see 7.2) then there are a number of other sources that can be consulted, but they are not comprehensive. If papers exist for a soldier who lost his life during the war it is possible that an Army Form B 2090A Field Service Report of Death of a Soldier may be found in his records. This form provides full service details together with the date and place of death and the cause.

13.1 Hospital Records

Hospital records held by the National Archives fall into four distinct types, each of which is described below.

First, all medical units serving overseas had to complete a unit war diary. These diaries can be found in WO 95 and are more fully explained in 7.2. Although the diaries provide a day-to-day account of the events concerning the medical unit, in many cases they also list the names of those who died whilst in their care, giving unit details and in many cases the cause of death. An example of a casualty list from a unit war diary can be seen in Fig. 51.

Secondly, the records held in MH 106 are a two per cent sample and represent the records used to compile an Official Medical History of the war (*History of the Great War based on Official Documents: Medical Services: Casualties and Medical Statistics of the Great War*). These records comprise three distinct groups: medical unit admission and discharge records; patient records; and records concerning certain types of wounds and diseases. There is a list of the medical unit records held in this record series at the beginning of the MH 106 catalogue. The medical units covered by these records include units

Figs. 40, 41 (overleaf and following page) *Admission Book for Craiglockhart Hospital recording Wilfred Owen's arrival and eventual discharge from the hospital.* MH 106/1887

Index number of admissions. Transfers are not to be numbered consecutively with the admissions, but should be left un-numbered, or numbered in red ink as a separate series	Regiment, Battalion, Corps, or other unit	Squadron, Battery, or Company	Regtl. No.	Rank	Surname	Christian Name	Age	Service	Completed months with Field Force	DISEASES (Wounds and injuries in action to be entered according to classification on fly leaf)
321^T	R.E.			Lt.	Tooley	C.E.	47	2 $\frac{7}{12}$	$\frac{2}{12}$	Neurasthenia
322^T	...wood For.			2 Lt.	Lewis	J.E.	40	1 $\frac{4}{12}$	$\frac{3}{12}$	Neurasthenia
323^T	..H.C.			Major	French	A.	48	21	1 $\frac{4}{12}$	Neurasthenia
324	8 K.R.R.			Lt.	Wright	A.	29	11yrs	1 $\frac{11}{12}$	Neurasthenia
325^T	R.E.			Lt.	Goodman	W.R.	27	2 $\frac{7}{12}$	$\frac{3}{12}$	Neurasthenia
326^T	R.g.a.			Lt.	Wells	J.L.	19	2 $\frac{4}{12}$	$\frac{7}{12}$	Neurasthenia
327^T	1 Wilts			2 Lt.	Bidwell	W.	24	2 $\frac{10}{12}$	1 $\frac{7}{12}$	Neurasthenia
328^T	R.R.R.			2 Lt.	Olivier	W.	24	2 $\frac{9}{12}$	$\frac{3}{12}$	Neurasthenia
329^T	M.g.c.			Lt.	Kirby	F.N.	24	2 $\frac{9}{12}$	1 $\frac{1}{12}$	Neurasthenia
330^T	2/6 K. L'pools			Capt.	Gilling	F.g.	39	2 $\frac{5}{12}$	$\frac{3}{12}$	Neurasthenia
331^T	16 R. Irish Regt.			2 Lt.	Lytton	J.H.	26	3 yrs	1 $\frac{3}{12}$	Neurasthenia
332^T	K.R.R.C.			2 Lt.	Wilkins	J.E.H.	22	6 yrs	$\frac{2}{12}$	Neurasthenia
333	24 R.F. att. 1st H.L.I.			Lt.	Kay	Granville	42	2 $\frac{9}{12}$	$\frac{3}{12}$	Neurasthenia
334^T	7 R.W. Kents			Lt.	Wills	Fred.W.	23	2 $\frac{4}{12}$	$\frac{2}{12}$	Neurasthenia
335^T	11th att. 2 S.R.			Lt.	Arnott	Wm.	29	2 $\frac{4}{12}$		Neurasthenia
336^T	2nd London			2 Lt.	Mackintosh	H.K.	30	1 $\frac{6}{12}$	$\frac{3}{12}$	Neurasthenia
337^T	1st Res. London Regt.			2 Lt.	Taylor	J.a.	24	2 $\frac{9}{12}$	$\frac{3}{12}$	Neurasthenia
338^T	2 K.O.S.B. Regt.			2 Lt.	Rhind	C.O.	29	8 yrs	1 $\frac{3}{12}$	Neurasthenia
339^T	a.S.G.			Lt.	Cann	W.R.	30	1 $\frac{6}{12}$	$\frac{4}{12}$	Neurasthenia
340^T	7th Norfolks			2 Lt.	Croker	F.g.	28	2 $\frac{8}{12}$	$\frac{6}{12}$	Neurasthenia
341^T	10th Lab.Co. & Devons			2 Lt.	Davison	T.V.J.	39	$\frac{3}{12}$	$\frac{3}{12}$	Neurasthenia
342^T	3 Sherwood For. att. 3 Lab.Coy.			2 Lt.	Butler	H.J.	25	2 yrs	$\frac{8}{12}$	Neurasthenia
343	R.E.			Cap.	De'ath	J.D.	24	4 yrs	2 $\frac{10}{12}$	Neurasthenia
344^T	4 W. Yorks			Cap.	Stevens	F.J.	35	15 yrs	$\frac{5}{12}$	Neurasthenia
345^T	R.g.a. 282 Siege B.y.			Major	Bingham	C.H.	30	10 $\frac{5}{12}$	2 $\frac{2}{12}$	Neurasthenia
346^T	S.W.B. att. a.Pr. Staff			Capt.	Master	R.a.	29	2 $\frac{8}{12}$	$\frac{10}{12}$	Neurasthenia
347^T	7th R.H.			2 Lt.	Salmond	J.B.	25	2 yrs	$\frac{9}{12}$	Neurasthenia
348^T	5th att. 2nd Manchesters			2 Lt.	Owen	W.E.S.	24	1 $\frac{7}{12}$	$\frac{6}{12}$	Neurasthenia
349^T	4th Camerons			Lieut.	MacEwen	J.M.	28	3 $\frac{4}{12}$	$\frac{3}{12}$	Neurasthenia
350^T	R.F.a.			2 Lt.	Lushington	C.F.	36	1 $\frac{7}{12}$	$\frac{7}{12}$	Neurasthenia

Date of Admission		Date of Discharge			Date of Transfer				Number of days under treatment	Number or designation of ward in which treated	Religion	OBSERVATIONS
For original disease	By new disease supervening	To Duty	By new disease supervening	By Death	To Sick Convoy	To Other Hospitals	From Sick Convoy	From Other Hospitals				Number and page of case book to be quoted for all cases recorded in it. In transfers the designation of the hospital or sick convoy, to which or from which transferred, must be noted here, and any other facts bearing on the man's destination; also in moveable field hospitals the place where the admission, &c., took place should be indicated. Place of action to be noted in case of wounds and injuries received in action.
$27\frac{10}{16}$		$13\frac{2}{18}$			4-7-17 Bowhill Re-ad. c.w.H. 24-7-17	23-7-17 3rd S.g. 24-7-17		4th S.g.H.	443		Pres.	
$27\frac{10}{16}$		$26\frac{4}{17}$ D.M.W.			Bowhill			"	89		C/E.	
$27\frac{10}{16}$		$13\frac{2}{17}$ D.M.W.						"	109		C/E.	
$27\frac{10}{16}$		$1\frac{12}{16}$ (on furlough)						"	35		C/E.	
$27\frac{10}{16}$		$21\frac{12}{16}$ (on leave)						"	55		C/E.	
$27\frac{10}{16}$		$10\frac{1}{17}$ (home service)						"	75		C/E.	
$27\frac{10}{16}$		$28\frac{3}{17}$ (D.M.W.)			7-1-17. Bowhill Re-ad. c.w.H. 19-2-17.	26-2-17.		"	152		C/E.	
$27\frac{10}{16}$					(Craighith) (accident)			"	115		Pres.	
$28\frac{10}{16}$		$1\frac{12}{16}$ (on furlough)						"	34		C/E.	
$30\frac{10}{16}$		$2\frac{1}{17}$ (to duty.)						"	64		C/E.	
$30\frac{10}{16}$		$17\frac{1}{17}$ (on furlough)						"	79		C/E.	
$30\frac{10}{16}$		—			9/12/16 Yorkhill			"	40		Pres.	
$3\frac{11}{16}$		$28\frac{12}{16}$ (on furlough)						"	55		C/E.	
$6\frac{11}{16}$		$18\frac{12}{16}$ (light duty)						"	42		C/E.	
$6\frac{11}{16}$		$12\frac{1}{17}$ (light duty)						"	67		C/E.	
$6\frac{11}{16}$		$22\frac{2}{17}$ (on furlough)			17-1-17. Bowhill Re-ad. c.w.H. 17-1-17	17-2-17. 17-2-17.		"	108		C/E.	
$6\frac{11}{16}$		$5\frac{3}{17}$ (D.M.W.)			Bowhill	Re-ad. c.w.H.		"	117		Pres.	
$10\frac{11}{16}$		$20\frac{12}{16}$ (home service)						"	40		C/E.	
$10\frac{11}{16}$		$16\frac{12}{16}$ (home service)						"	36		C/E.	
$14\frac{11}{16}$		$28\frac{2}{17}$ (to duty)			17-1-17. Bowhill Re-ad. c.w.H. (Bowhill again 28/7/17.)	22-2-17.		"	106		Pres.	
$18\frac{11}{16}$		$19\frac{12}{16}$ (light duty)						4th S.g.	31		C/E.	
$19\frac{11}{16}$		$5\frac{4}{17}$ (lab. bn. abroad)						4th S.g.	137		C/E.	
$20\frac{11}{16}$		$19\frac{12}{16}$ (D.M.W.)					1/1/12	1st S.g.	28		Pres.	Disch. 1st S.g. 1/4/12. Home & light duty since till admission to c.w.H.
$23\frac{11}{16}$											C/E.	
$28\frac{11}{16}$		$18\frac{1}{17}$ (on furlough)						4th S.g.	51		C/E.	
$30\frac{11}{16}$		$10\frac{4}{17}$ D.M.W.						Yorkhill	131		Pres.	
$1\frac{12}{16}$		$30\frac{13}{16}$ (to duty.)						4th S.g.	30		R.C.	
$2\frac{12}{16}$		$28\frac{3}{17}$ (home service)			24-1-17. Bowhill Re-ad.c.w	4-3-17 Yorkhill			126		Pres.	
$23\frac{11}{16}$		$22\frac{2}{17}$ (gar. duty abroad)						2nd S.g.	119		C/E.	
$7\frac{12}{16}$					2-2-17 Craighouse	Yorkhill			57		Pres.	

Fig. 42 *Field Service notification of the death of an officer.* WO 339/37823

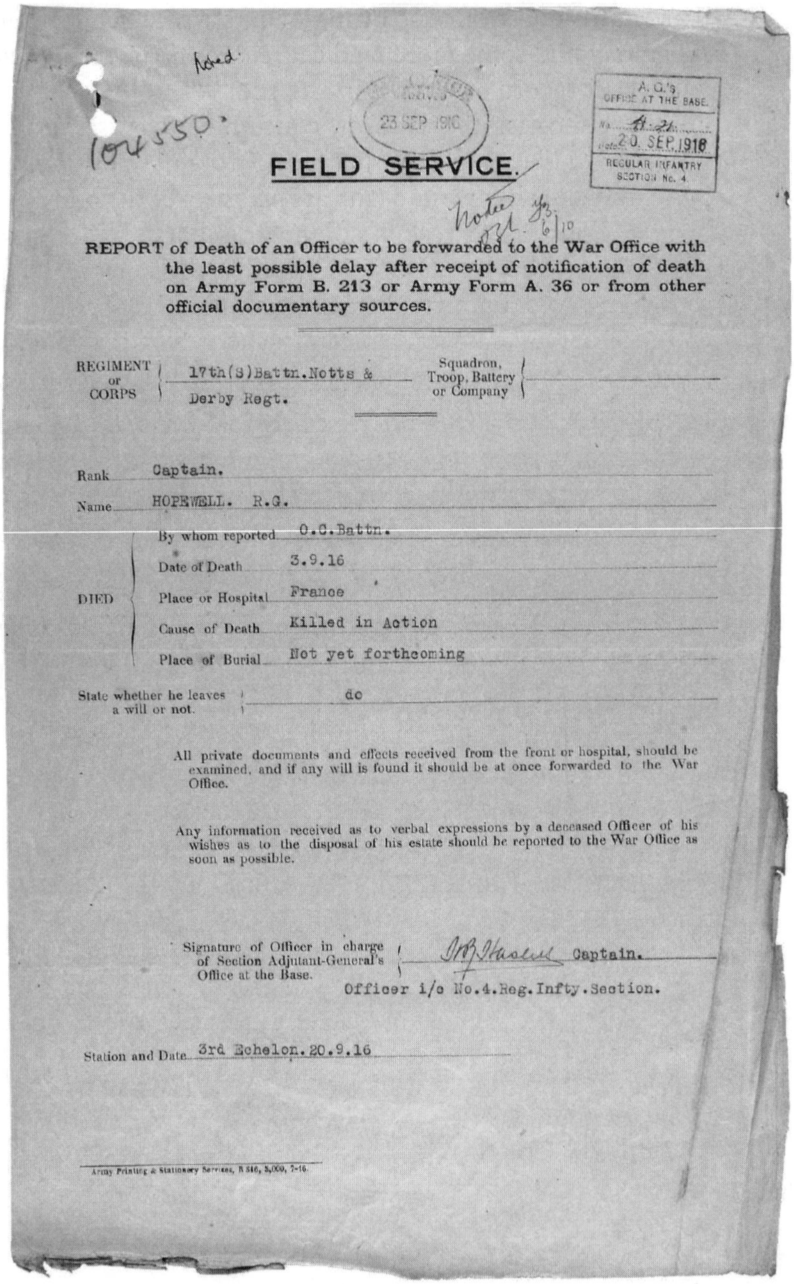

104550.

A. G.'s OFFICE AT THE BASE. No. 8.21. Date 20 SEP 1916 REGULAR INFANTRY SECTION No. 4.

23 SEP 1916

FIELD SERVICE.

REPORT of Death of an Officer to be forwarded to the War Office with the least possible delay after receipt of notification of death on Army Form B. 213 or Army Form A. 36 or from other official documentary sources.

REGIMENT or CORPS: 17th(S)Battn.Notts & Derby Regt.

Squadron, Troop, Battery or Company:

Rank: Captain.

Name: HOPEWELL. R.G.

DIED
By whom reported: O.C.Battn.
Date of Death: 3.9.16
Place or Hospital: France
Cause of Death: Killed in Action
Place of Burial: Not yet forthcoming

State whether he leaves a will or not: do

All private documents and effects received from the front or hospital, should be examined, and if any will is found it should be at once forwarded to the War Office.

Any information received as to verbal expressions by a deceased Officer of his wishes as to the disposal of his estate should be reported to the War Office as soon as possible.

Signature of Officer in charge of Section Adjutant-General's Office at the Base. Captain.
Officer i/c No.4.Reg.Infty.Section.

Station and Date: 3rd Echelon. 20.9.16

that served at home and/or overseas.

Thirdly, the patient records are split into unit records and records organized by wound type. The units covered by MH 106 include the Royal Horse Artillery, a number of Hussar Regiments, the Grenadier Guards, the Leicester Regiment and the Royal Flying Corps. These unit records are arranged in case sheet number. If you know that an individual from one of these units was wounded during the war, you may find some more medical records apart from those preserved with their record of service, in MH 106.

Amongst the records concerning diseases and wounds can be found files on patients suffering from gas poisoning, bayonet wounds and gun shot wounds in various parts of the body.

Fourthly, the admission and discharge books in MH 106 represent only a small number of medical units from home and overseas. Preserved amongst the collection in MH 106 is the admission register for Craiglockhart Hospital where Siegfried Sassoon and Wilfred Owen were both patients. An example of an admission register can be seen in Figs. 40 and 41.

13.2   Disability Pensions

The most significant collection of papers concerning disability pensions are the records in PIN 26. Information about these records can be found in 2.8 for officers, 3.6 for other ranks and 4.3 for nurses.

There are a number of records series created by the Paymaster General that contain information about payments made to officers.

The arrangement of each volume in the following series is broadly similar; some are indexed, others are not. Nearly all of the volumes give the name, rank and regiment of the individual. They tell you how much money was to be paid, how frequently (usually quarterly) and to whom. In the case of dependants, it will usually give their relationship to the officer. Most of the records state when a payment was to start, under what authority (usually a warrant) it was granted and when the payments ceased. Addresses are frequently to be found amongst the records.

The following PMG series and specific pieces may be of interest.

PMG 9 PENSIONS OR GRATUITIES FOR WOUNDS
    PMG 9/53–66

PMG 42 DISABILITY RETIRED PAY AND GRATUITIES
    PMG 42/1–12

PMG 43 SUPPLEMENTARY ALLOWANCES AND SPECIAL GRANTS
    PMG 43/2 only

13.3 War Dead

There are two major secondary sources available in the National Archives that can provide data about those men and women who died during the war, whether they were killed in action, died of wounds or disease, an accident or even natural causes. *Soldiers Died in the Great War* and *Officers Died in the Great War* list those who died during the war, and provide unit details, place and date of death and in many cases other unit details if they had served in another unit from that in which they died. Originally arranged by unit and then in alphabetical order, now that both of these works are available on CD-ROM it is possible to do a simple name search. *Soldiers* is also available on microfilm, and *Officers* in book form. Both of these sources only cover deaths between 4 August 1914 and 11 November 1918.

Access to *Soldiers Died* and *Officers Died in the Great War* is available on any of the public computers at the National Archives via the 'Published and Online Resources' link (OPERA).

Weekly casualty returns of Indian Army officers are held by the British Library under the reference L/MIL/14/139–140. An alphabetical list of Indian Army officer casualties giving name, rank, unit, date and place of death and cause can be found in L/MIL/14/142.

The Commonwealth War Graves Commission (formerly the Imperial War Graves Commission) has a computerized database of all of those men and women who lost their lives during the two World Wars and, unlike *Soldiers* and *Officers Died*, the database covers those who died from after 11 November 1918, whose death could be attributed to war service. This database is available on the internet at *www.cwgc.org*. Access to the Commonwealth War Graves Commission website can be made at the National Archives and printouts of individual entries can be obtained.

13.4 Deceased Soldiers' Effects

When a soldier died in service, in whatever circumstances, the Army would endeavour to ensure that his estate and certain personal effects were returned to the next of kin. The records concerning deceased soldiers' effects for the First World War are held by the National Army Museum and the information they contain includes name, rank and number, unit, place of death (usually the operational theatre), date of death, financial value of estate and to whom it was passed. Unfortunately, at the time of writing these records were not accessible. However, the National Army Museum do carry our searches of

Fig. 43 *A statistical analysis of casualties in Cameroon.* WO 32/5327

Table
Appendix 8.

I N V A L I D S.
(British to 21.2.16 (1378 invalided on 21.2.16) French to 19.2.16)

	EUROPEANS		NATIVE SOLDIERS		CARRIERS	
	British	French	British	French	British	French
Enteric Fever	-	6	-	-	-	-
Chicken Pox	-	-	-	-	15	-
Beri-Beri...	-	-	4	255	-	56
Blackwater..	2	5	-	-	-	-
Malaria	19	128	11	22	68	17
Leprosy	-	-	5	-	-	-
Dysentery...	13	34	22	55	749	154
Major Septic	-	-	3	3	-	4
Tropical Ulcers... ...	-	-	80	46	2500	1476
Other Minor Septic ...	9	1	41	20	144	43
Pneumonia...	-	1	14	35	416	30
Rheumatism..	-	2	49	-	324	-
Tubercle of Lungs ...	2	-	16	47	5	3
Venereal	-	5	11	55	94	25
Guinea Worm.	-	-	17	30	268	31
Wasting	-	-	-	-	630	-
Anaemia	51	81	16	83	33	188
Debility	1	-	22	-	802	-
Physically Unfit. ...	-	-	-	-	265	-
Nervous	17	5	21	9	13	1
Eye	2	4	18	57	35	6
Ear	1	2	5	1	-	-
Heart..	3	-	42	-	150	-
Respiratory.	1	13	25	73	626	65
Digestive...	23	17	37	-	67	-
Generative..	-	-	27	-	129	-
Urinary	2	5	15	6	9	-
Hernia.	1	-	29	13	145	2
Skin...	2	3	13	-	175	-
Organs of Locomotion..	6	6	-	53	-	36
Local Injuries... ...	5	-	21	61	51	19
Wounds in Action. ...	15	25	121	64	-	8
Sunstroke...	1	-	-	2	-	-
	176	343	685	990	7713	2164

D E A T H S.
Analysis of 459 of the 720 Deaths from Disease among Europeans and Natives of the Allied Forces.

Enteric Fever..	6	Heart..	5
Dysentery.	176	Beri-Beri...	12
Blackwater	5	Syphilis	1
Malaria...	13	Digestive...	31
Pneumonia.	156	Local Injuries... ...	10
Tuberculosis...	4	P.U.O.	1
Bronchitis	17	Hernia	1
Pleurisy..	3	Nervous	5
Haemoptysis	1	Rheumatism..	2
Major Septic...	8	Urinary	1
		Connective Tissue ...	1
			459

these records, for which they charge a fee of £10. For further information contact the National Army Museum at the address given in 15.3.4.

In the case of officers who died during the war, details concerning their estates can usually be found in their records of service, if they have survived. See chapter 2 for further details.

13.5 Widows' and Dependants' Pensions

Brief details concerning the pensions paid to a number of widows whose husbands died between 1914 and 1918 can be found in PIN 82.

PIN 82 consists of 183 separate pieces, each listing 50 servicemen.

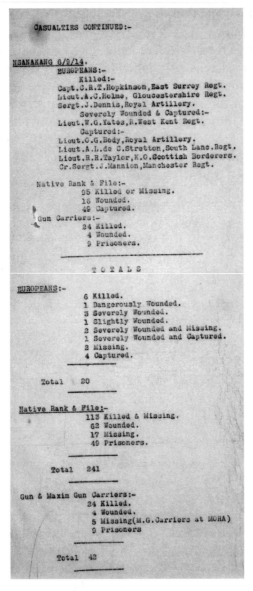

Fig. 44 *Casualty details contained in a Military Headquarters report for operations in West Africa.*
WO 158/571

CASUALTIES CONTINUED:-

NSANAKANG 6/9/14.

    EUROPEANS:-
        Killed:-
        Capt.C.R.T.Hopkinson,East Surrey Regt.
        Lieut.A.C.Holme, Gloucestershire Regt.
        Sergt.J.Dennis,Royal Artillery.
            Severely Wounded & Captured:-
        Lieut.W.G.Yates,R.West Kent Regt.
            Captured:-
        Lieut.O.G.Body,Royal Artillery.
        Lieut.A.L.de C.Stretton,South Lanc.Regt.
        Lieut.R.R.Taylor,K.O.Scottish Borderers.
        Cr.Sergt.J.Mannion,Manchester Regt.

    Native Rank & File:-
        95 Killed or Missing.
        16 Wounded.
        49 Captured.
    Gun Carriers:-
        24 Killed.
        4 Wounded.
        9 Prisoners.

                T O T A L S

EUROPEANS:-
            6 Killed.
            1 Dangerously Wounded.
            3 Severely Wounded.
            1 Slightly Wounded.
            2 Severely Wounded and Missing.
            1 Severely Wounded and Captured.
            2 Missing.
            4 Captured.

        Total   20

Native Rank & File:-
            113 Killed & Missing.
            62 Wounded.
            17 Missing.
            49 Prisoners.

        Total   241

Gun & Maxim Gun Carriers:-
            24 Killed.
            4 Wounded.
            5 Missing(M.G.Carriers at MORA)
            9 Prisoners

        Total   42

They provide very basic service data about the deceased, including unit data, date and place of death, and information about the widow and any children, including place of residence and the amount of pension they were granted. A list of names of those whose details can be found in PIN 82 can be found at the beginning of the PIN 82 catalogue. It is also possible to search the PIN 82 series by name of widow or deceased on the Catalogue.

A different collection of widows' pensions can be found in PIN 26/17179–19720. These files are arranged by name of the deceased.

A small collection of files of dependants' pensions can be found in

PIN 26/19821–19853 and are arranged by name of dependant (usually children).

A number of records created and kept by the Paymaster General, containing the details of payments made to officers' widows and other dependants, can be found in the following records series. The arrangement of the records is broadly similar, with most containing an index. The information in each volume provides the name, rank and regiment of the officer, the amount to be paid, to whom and how often. The address of the recipient of the money and their relationship to the officer is frequently given.

PMG 44 PENSIONS TO RELATIVES OF DECEASED OFFICERS
PMG 44/1–7

PMG 45 WIDOW'S PENSIONS
PMG 45/1–6

PMG 46 CHILDREN'S ALLOWANCES
PMG 46/1–4

PMG 47 RELATIVES OF MISSING OFFICERS
PMG 47/1–3

13.6 The Memorial Plaque and Scroll

At the end of the war, the next of kin of all those men and women who had lost their lives during the war — or whose death was attributed to war service up to seven years after the war had ended (11 November 1925) — were given a memorial plaque and scroll bearing the full name of the deceased. The plaque is often called the 'Dead Man's Penny' or 'Death Plaque'.

13.7 Other Printed Rolls

There are numerous published casualty rolls and other rolls of honour. Many casualty rolls can be found on the internet.

Examples of rolls held by the National Archives include the rolls of honour of the Midland Railway (RAIL 491/1259), the London, Brighton and South Coast Railway (RAIL 414/791) and the North Eastern Railway (RAIL 527/993).

Information concerning the officers who were killed during the Gallipoli operations can be found in *To What End Did They Die:*

Officers Who Died at Gallipoli by R.W. Walker.

A published list of all those killed on the first day of the battle of the Somme, 1 July 1916, can be found in E.W. Bell (ed.) *Soldiers Killed on the First Day of the Somme* (1977), a copy of which is in the National Archives Library.

Other published works available at the National Archives include the *Cross of Sacrifice* series by D.B. and S.B. Jarvis, which lists casualties by service, rank and in alphabetical order, giving date of death and place of commemoration.

The *National Roll of Honour 1914–1918*, published in 14 volumes in the years after the war, covers the dead of a number of towns around the United Kingdom. Unusually, the roll also includes those who survived the war. A copy of this work is available in the National Archives Library, at the Imperial War Museum and at the Society of Genealogists, and was republished by Naval and Military Press in 2001.

Although not a roll as such, information regarding all of those officers of the rank of brigadier general or above who died or were wounded or captured, can be found in *Bloody Red Tabs* by F. Davies and G. Maddocks.

A small number of rolls of honour from other government departments can be found at the National Archives by searching the Catalogue using the term 'roll of honour'.

13.8 Death Certificates

Death certificates for service personnel who died during the war can be obtained from the General Registry Office. See 15.3.5.

14 RECORDS OF THE DOMINION FORCES

The records of service of members of the armed forces of the Dominions—Australia, Canada, New Zealand and South Africa—are held by their respective national archives or appropriate government bodies. During the First World War the forces of these countries were considered by many to be the best troops in the British Army. However, many of the men who saw service in the forces of the Dominions were either British by birth or had British origins.

When requesting information from overseas please provide as much information about the individual as possible. Name, rank and number, if known, will really help.

14.1 Operational Records

Although the Dominions kept their own operational records, many of which are preserved in their own archives, there are basic unit war diaries preserved in the National Archives in the record series WO 95.

The unit war diaries held in the Library and Archives Canada are more complete than those held in the National Archives in as much as they have many of the personnel records which regiments were obliged to keep still with the diaries. It is therefore possible to find information concerning leave, sickness, promotions and postings. See 14.4 for more information on the Library and Archives Canada.

For more information about operational records, see chapter 7.

14.2 Records of Service at the National Archives

Although there are no generic collections of records of service for men of the Dominions, there are a number of files concerning British men who joined one of the Dominion forces in WO 364. These men are likely either to have joined the Dominions' forces in the UK or to have been medically discharged and then to have opted to remain in

the UK rather than return to the Dominion they had served. More information about the individuals in either of these situations can be found in chapter 3.

14.3 Records of Service and Operational Records: Australia

Records of service of the Australian Imperial Forces (AIF) are held by the National Archives of Australia in Canberra. It is possible to obtain copies from Australia and information concerning the records and a search service can be found on the Australian National Archives website, *www.naa.gov.au*. The postal address to write to for these records is:

First World War Personnel Record Service
National Archives of Australia
PO Box 7425
Canberra Mail Centre ACT 2610
Australia
Email: *ref@naa.gov.au*
Tel: 1300 886 882

Fig. 45 *Canadian infantrymen returning from the front line at the Battle of the Somme in 1916.*

To access the information on the National Archives of Australia website, the following navigational information may help:

Click on *www.naa.gov.au*
Click on Collection
Click on Explore
Click on Defence
Click on Conflicts
Click on World War 1:1914–1918
Click on Army–World War 1
Scroll down for Service Dossiers and enlistment applications
Click on First Australian Imperial Forces personnel dossiers (World War service records)
or click on Applications to enlist in the Australian Imperial Force

The Australian War Memorial (AWM), also in Canberra, has a number of very useful resources, most of which are online at *www.awm.gov.au*.

Of the databases held by the AWM two are really useful: a Roll of Honour listing those members of the AIF who lost their lives and a Nominal Roll that lists those members of the AIF who went overseas. Both of these resources can be accessed by following this navigational advice:

Click on Biographical Databases

There are a number of different resources available via this page:

Click on 'Research a Person' for access to a search mechanism which you can populate with the name of the individual and the conflict in which they served. The search will then signpost likely resources.
Click on 'Roll of Honour' for details of those Australians who died in the First World War.
Click on 'Nominal Rolls' for lists of Australians who served in the First World War.
Click on 'Honours and Awards' for access to lists of *Gazetted* awards to Australian service personnel and also the actual recommendations for awards for the First World War period. The recommendations can be downloaded as PDF files.
Off the 'Collections' icon on the home page you can access the Australian Imperial Force unit war diaries.
Click on 'War Diaries', then 'First World War', where there are 35 different classes, not all of which have so far been digitized. Class

23, for example, is 'Infantry', where you can look at the diaries at 'brigade' or 'battalion' level.

14.4   Records of Service and Operational Records: Canada

The records of service of the Canadian Expeditionary Force (CEF) are held by the Library and Archives Canada in Ottawa (*www.archives.ca*). The first contingent of the CEF arrived in Britain in October 1914. A significant number of British men joined the CEF after it arrived in the UK simply because prior to 1916 entry into the British Army was still voluntary and the CEF offered better conditions and, most importantly, better pay.

Information concerning the records of the CEF can be obtained by writing to the following address:

Personnel Records Unit
Library and Archives Canada
395 Wellington Street
Ottawa ON
K1A ON3
Canada

Information about the CEF records is also available online at *www.collectionscanada.gc.ca*.

To access the information about the CEF records online the following navigational information may help:

Click on *www.collectionscanada.gc.ca*
Click on English
Click on Canadian Genealogy Centre
Under 'Most Requested Records' click on Military
Click on First World War
Click on Soldiers of the First World War database
Click on Search

The database can be searched using the fields surname, given name(s) and regimental number(s). The results page will give you the name, date of birth of an individual, rank, regimental number(s) and the actual document reference for the papers. If you click on the name of the individual it will enable you to download the front and back pages of the record for free. This is especially useful if you are unsure about an individual, as it will help you to identify them more clearly.

Fig. 46 *ANZAC soldiers resting on their way up to the trenches at the Somme in 1916.*

To access the Canadian Expeditionary Force unit war diaries follow the same links as given above, but from the 'Military' page click on 'War Diaries'.

The 'War Diaries' page will lead you to a number of options, including 'Unit War Diaries of the First World War'. The next page will lead you to a searchable database of units that can be searched by unit identity, full date or year only.

Information about other records relevant to Canada and the First World War can also be found from the 'First World War' page mentioned above.

Another large collection of military records held in Ottawa is the records of service of the Newfoundland Regiment. These records are in a separate collection as Newfoundland did not become part of Canada until 1947.

Among the other records held in Canada are what are known as 'Imperial War Service Gratuities', which include land grants given to former members of the British Army—primarily Britons who wished to settle in Canada. The information contained in these records includes a detailed synopsis of their military careers.

Fig. 47 *A battery of the Hong Kong and Singapore Artillery in action during the First Battle of Gaza in 1917.*

For information about entitlement to campaign medals for the First World War, it is necessary to write to:

Honours and Awards Section
Veterans Affairs Canada
66 Slater Street
Ottawa, ON
KIA OP4

14.5 Records of Service and Operational Records: New Zealand

The military records of service of the New Zealand Expeditionary Force are held by the Archives of New Zealand. The Archives hold 122,357 files for individuals who served in the First World War, but approximately 6,000 files are still held by the New Zealand Defence Forces for those personnel who served after 1920.

It is possible to search for individual's papers on the Archives of New Zealand website via the 'Archway' (*www.archway.archives.govt.nz*).

If you find an appropriate reference you can order a copy (payment in advance) from:

reference@archives.govt.nz
Access Services
Archives New Zealand
PO 12 050
Wellington

The Archives of New Zealand also hold the NZ Expeditionary Forces unit war diary, but they have yet to be digitized.

If you wish to visit Archives New Zealand you will need to go to the Wellington Office at:

10 Mulgrave Street
Thorndon
Wellington
6011
New Zealand
Website: *www.archives.govt.nz*

The records of service personnel who served after 1920 are still with the NZ Defence Forces. Some brief information is available on the internet at *www.army.mil.nz*. Click on 'Culture and History' then 'Personnel Archives'.

14.6   Records of Service: South Africa

Surviving military records of service of men who saw service in the South African Forces during the First World War are held at the National Archives of South Africa. Searches can be carried out by contacting the following address:

Military Information Bureau
National Archives of South Africa
Private Bag X289
Pretoria 0001
South Africa

15 RECORDS HELD OUTSIDE THE NATIONAL ARCHIVES

The National Archives is not the only archive that preserves information about the First World War. Although the records of service and operational records are important, many other papers can be found at institutions around the United Kingdom.

15.1 Absent Voters Lists

Many people attempting to discover the record of service of an individual who saw service in the First World War have no idea as to their service details. Of all the records held outside the National Archives, the absent voters lists can provide that essential data.

By an Act of Parliament passed in February 1918, servicemen were allowed to register in order to be able to obtain a vote in their home constituency. These absent voter lists can provide name, rank, number, unit and home address of each soldier registered.

The lists are not held by the National Archives, but are dispersed locally in the various archives of the counties and boroughs relevant to the areas the lists cover. The British Library has a small collection, but it is best to start at the County Record Office of the area where the soldier was registered to vote.

A number of absent voters lists can be found on the internet. By searching for the place name in conjunction with absent voters lists, you will find some.

15.2 Newspapers

Of all the records produced during the First World War, national and local newspapers are a most underrated source. Depending upon the unit, information about the personnel in it would quite often reach the press. Apart from casualty lists, which were published in *The Times*, information concerning local units — such as 'Pals' units —

frequently appeared in local newspapers. Information about gallantry awards and promotions quite often appeared, as did photographs of many soldiers.

Copies of old local newspapers are often held by local libraries and the best collection of newspapers, both national and local, is held by the British Library at Colindale, see 15.3.2.

Access to *The Times Online* is available at the National Archives and you can access the resource from any public computer. It is possible to search *The Times Online* by name or keyword and to set the date parameters for the search. Anything you do find can be downloaded and printed.

15.3 Other Archives

Other archives where records concerning the First World War may be found include the following:

15.3.1 *Imperial War Museum*

The Imperial War Museum (IWM) has departments holding documents, printed books, photographs and oral history. Access to these records is by appointment.

For those with an interest in war memorials, the IWM holds the

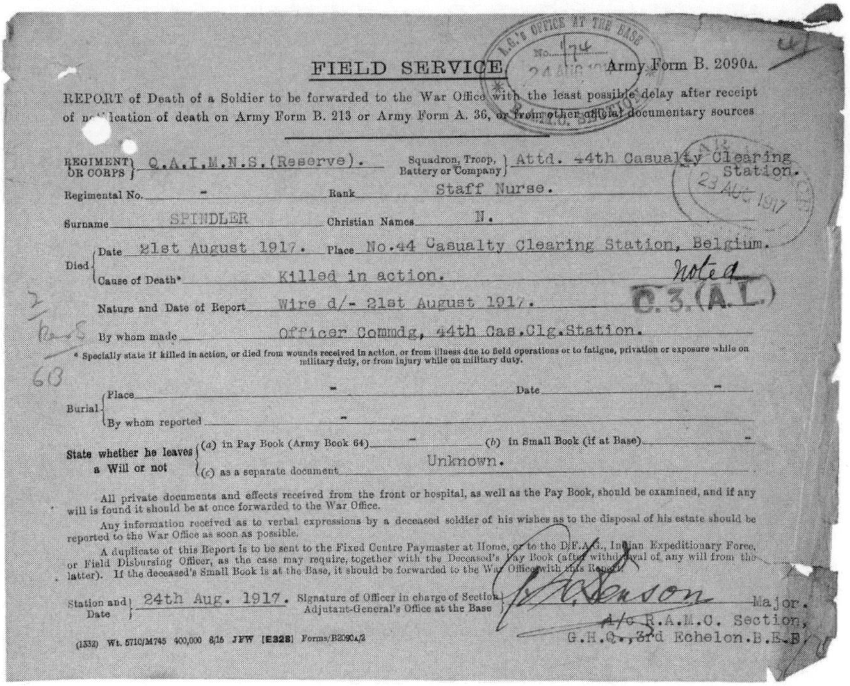

FIELD SERVICE. Army Form B. 2090A.

REPORT of Death of a Soldier to be forwarded to the War Office with the least possible delay after receipt of notification of death on Army Form B. 213 or Army Form A. 36, or from other official documentary sources

REGIMENT OR CORPS: Q.A.I.M.N.S.(Reserve). Squadron, Troop, Battery or Company: Attd. 44th Casualty Clearing Station.

Regimental No.: - Rank: Staff Nurse.

Surname: SPINDLER Christian Names: N.

Died: Date: 21st August 1917. Place: No.44 Casualty Clearing Station, Belgium.

Cause of Death*: Killed in action.

Nature and Date of Report: Wire d/- 21st August 1917.

By whom made: Officer Commdg, 44th Cas.Clg.Station.

* Specially state if killed in action, or died from wounds received in action, or from illness due to field operations or to fatigue, privation or exposure while on military duty, or from injury while on military duty.

Burial: Place: - Date: -

By whom reported: -

State whether he leaves a Will or not: (a) in Pay Book (Army Book 64): - (b) in Small Book (if at Base): -

(c) as a separate document: Unknown.

All private documents and effects received from the front or hospital, as well as the Pay Book, should be examined, and if any will is found it should be at once forwarded to the War Office.

Any information received as to verbal expressions by a deceased soldier of his wishes as to the disposal of his estate should be reported to the War Office as soon as possible.

A duplicate of this Report is to be sent to the Fixed Centre Paymaster at Home, or to the D.F.A.G., Indian Expeditionary Force, or Field Disbursing Officer, as the case may require, together with the Deceased's Pay Book (after withdrawal of any will from the latter). If the deceased's Small Book is at the Base, it should be forwarded to the War Office with this Report.

Station and Date: 24th Aug. 1917. Signature of Officer in charge of Section Adjutant-General's Office at the Base: Major. A/c R.A.M.C. Section, G.H.Q., 3rd Echelon.B.E.F.

(1332) Wt. 5710/M745 400,000 8/16 JFW [E328] Forms/B2090A/2

noted

C.3.(A.L.)

Fig. 48 *Field Service notification of the death of Staff Nurse Nellie Spindler.* WO 399/7850

Fig. 49 *British cavalry resting whilst waiting for a breakthrough during the Battle of Arras.*

National Inventory of War Memorials. Further information can be found at *www.ukniwm.org.uk*.

The Imperial War Museum
Lambeth Road
London
SE1 6HZ
Tel: 020 7416 5000
Website: *www.iwm.org.uk*

15.3.2 *British Library*
The British Library holds the records of the India Office, including records of the Indian Army. Access is by reader's ticket, which can be obtained on the ground floor.

The British Library
Oriental and India Office Collection
96 Euston Road

London
NW1 2DR
Tel: 020 7412 7873
Website: *www.bl.uk*

The British Library also has a newspaper library at Colindale in north London. Many of the papers held at Colindale are available on microfilm, and many are now being digitized. For further information about the Newspaper Library see the British Library website or write to:

The British Library Newspaper Library
Colindale Avenue
London
NW9 5HE
Tel: 020 7412 7353

15.3.3   *Commonwealth War Graves Commission*
The Commonwealth War Graves Commission (CWGC) holds the cemetery registers and memorial registers for all of the graves and memorials for which it is responsible. There is no public access. If you have access to the internet, the CWGC Database is available online. Access is also available at the National Archives.

The Commonwealth War Graves Commission
2 Marlow Road
Maidenhead
Berkshire
SL6 7DX
Tel: 01628 634221
Website: *www.cwgc.org*

15.3.4   *National Army Museum*
The National Army Museum holds a number of manuscript sources concerning the First World War and a number of regimental collections, including the Middlesex Regiment. Access to the National Army Museums Templer Study Centre is by reader's ticket.

The National Army Museum
Royal Hospital Road
Chelsea
London
SW3 4HT

Tel: 020 7730 0717
Website: *www.national-army-museum.ac.uk*

15.3.5 *General Registry Office*
The General Registry Office (GRO) in London closed in 2007, and it is now only possible to search their registers and order certificates via the internet or telephone. Access to the GRO's registers of War Dead is available via their website on the public computers at the National Archives, but it is not possible to order copies at Kew.

Tel: 0845 603 7788 (certificate enquiries)
Email: *certificate.services@ons.gsi.gov.uk*
Website: *www.gro.gov.uk*

It is possible to search the indexes for births, marriages and deaths via the Find My Past website (*www.findmypast.com*), a link to which can be found on the public computer terminals at Kew. To access Find My Past use the 'Records and Documents' icon and then scroll down to 'Birth, marriages & deaths 1837–2005'. Click on the link and then you will be able to search.

15.3.6 *British Red Cross Museum and Archives*
Access to the Red Cross Archives is by appointment. Among the records held by the Red Cross are the records of Voluntary Aid detachment personnel.

British Red Cross
UK Office
44 Moorfields
London
EC2Y 9AL
Tel: 0844 871 1111
Email: *enquiry@redcross.org.uk*
Website: *www.redcross.org.uk*

15.3.7 *Regimental Museums and Archives*
Accessing the archives of the corps and regiments of the British Army requires perhaps greater patience than using the records at national level. There are a number of reasons for this, the main one being availability. Not all regiments hold their archives at their museums. Some are in the museum, some at the Regimental Headquarters, others under local authority care or in an archive or museum you least expect.

Fig. 50 (facing) *British troops moving from a reserve trench to the front line near Tilloy-les-Mofflaines during the battle of Arras.*

The most efficient way to locate regimental archive collections is to use *Military Museums in the UK*, as this book will provide you with the contact data for each museum or collection.

Many regimental archives have few resources to carry out research and rely heavily on volunteers and overworked staff whose tasks are many. An initial letter (with a SAE) or phone call asking how to proceed with your research will usually pay dividends.

Another route to military museums is, of course, the internet. Many regimental museums have their own websites and these can be found by using a search engine, the MOD website *www.mod.uk* or the Army Museums Ogilby Trust website *www.armymuseums.org.uk*.

Since the end of the First World War many regiments have been disbanded or amalgamated with others, and it may take you time to identify the current identity of a First World War period regiment in order to locate their old records. A useful way to identify current unit identities and their origins is to use the British Army website and look under the heading of 'Units'.

15.3.8 *First Aid Nursing Yeomanry*

Although members of the First Aid Nursing Yeomanry (FANY) who received campaign medals will be mentioned in the medal records in WO 372 and WO 329, other records relating to their service are held elsewhere. For further information about the FANY records contact:

FANY (PRVC)
TA Centre
95 Horseferry Road
London SW1P 2DX
Tel: 020 7976 5459
Email: *hq@fany.org.uk*
Website: *www.fany.org.uk*

15.3.9 *St John Ambulance*

The Museum and Library of the Order of St John is another source of information about individuals who saw service in the Order.

The Museum of the Order of St John
St John's Gate
St John's Lane
London EC1M 4DA
Tel: 020 7324 4005
Website: *www.sja.org.uk*

16 RESEARCH TECHNIQUES

As there are millions of records of service and individual medal records, so the permutations are almost limitless. There are, however, a number of different ways to approach the records, depending upon what sort of information you seek.

16.1 How to Begin

Due to the sheer numbers of men and women who served in the British Army during the period 1914–18, unless you have something that sets one individual apart from another, your research may not achieve the desired results.

The most significant item to start with is the name. People have appeared at the National Archives with a photograph of a First World War period soldier, with no name and the soldier having no badges to identify his regiment or rank. The only answer to a photograph like this is 'yes, it's a 1902 pattern uniform' or words to that effect!

The following facts will help you at the start of your research, and whilst they seem obvious, they really do help:

> Name
> Status (Officer or Other Rank)
> Regiment or Corps
> Regimental number (Other Ranks only)

Unless the individual had a very unusual forename or surname, finding the correct individual when they have a common forename and surname, may require additional information to that listed above.

What is needed to separate one individual with a common name from another soldier of the same name is what I have always called a 'unique identifier'. Items of specific personal information, such as a date and place of birth, name of parents, wife, home address, names of children or employer, can all be used as a 'unique identifier'.

There are lots of potential sources for the basic items of informa-

7th Bn. The Queens Regt. **App C₂**

CASUALTY LIST FROM 6·7·17 to 24·7·17

OFFICERS KILLED

Captain HEDLEY JOHN A'BEAR   10·7·17
2/Lieut. ALBERT JOHN FRANCIS OSBORNE 10·7·17
2/Lieut. CHARLES HAROLD MASON   6·7·17

O.R. KILLED

'A' Coy.
NIL.

'B' Coy.
6494   Pte.   ALSTON. A   11·7·17
13365   "   GLOVER. J   13·7·17
13114   "   CARPENTER. H.   13·7·17
959   "   FARMER. J.   20·7·17
206923 Sergt. BOX. J.C.   23·7·17
11278 L/Cpl. STOTTER. W.G.   23·7·17
22859 Pte.   HINDLE. E.   23·7·17

'C' Coy.
24703 L/Sergt. PALMER. S.   16·7·17
17794 L/Cpl. DUNN. W.   16·7·17
14931 Pte.   ETCHELLS. F.   16·7·17

2.

O.R. KILLED
'C' Coy. (contd.)
15919. Pte. JEFFREY. J.   16·7·17
37745   "   GOODWIN. H.   16·7·17
21805   "   EDGINGTON. R.   14·7·17
21195   "   PRESS. B.   16·7·17

'D' Coy.
37753 Pte. HAMPTON. F.   13·7·17
12049   "   WHITTICK. W. J.   14·7·17
8350   "   BURFORD. T.E.   14·7·17
3701   "   WOOD. J.R.   14·7·17
15714   "   WHITTON. G.   14·7·17
29160   "   PRATT. J.   17·7·17
683525 "   GOODALL. T.H.   21·7·17

H.Q. Coy.
NIL.

O.R. WOUNDED.
6863. Pte. WINTER. A.   10·7·17
681052   "   TURNER. T.   10·7·17
9525   "   ERRINGTON. L.   9·7·17
37126   "   MILLER.   11·7·17
39086   "   ALLEN. F.   11·7·17
6987   "   STREETLY. F.S.   9·7·17

Fig. 51 *A very detailed casualty list for 7 Queens (Royal West Surrey) Regiment for July 1917.* WO 95/2051

tion required to use the records more effectively. The following are places to start looking:

Medals: If you have any First World War medals, they are usually named around the edge or on the back. The medals will give you all that you need to start your research.

Certificates: Many ordinary soldiers got married in a hurry before they went overseas. Get a copy of the marriage certificate. Any children born between 1914 and 1919 to a soldier may record his service details on the birth certificate. Any officer commissioned during the war would have received a commission warrant with the rank and regiment recorded on it.

Photographs: Many soldiers had their photographs taken before they went overseas or at some time after they had arrived in France. Depending upon the image, you may find all you need is in the photograph: the regiment/corps and the rank. If you can, look at the back of the photograph—it may have the name of the person if you don't know that already. Many units had group photographs of the men within the unit taken at home or overseas at some time during the war. Some of these photographs were used in regimental histories published after the war.

Correspondence: Letters, either personal or official, are a useful source. Letters sent with campaign medals, the boxes the medals were sent in, field postcards and the dreaded telegrams or letters sent to inform the next of kin of the death of a soldier may provide some useful information.

Other items: Identity (Dog) tags record the name, number, religion and regiment/corps of a soldier. Bibles carried by individuals sometimes have informative inscriptions in. Newspapers of the period, especially local ones, frequently carried letters from the Front, articles about people joining up and, unfortunately, the death notices and obituaries of those who died.

16.2 Joining the Army

The process of joining the Army is not relevant to the purpose of this guide, but some basic information about joining the Army may be useful.

Once war was declared thousands of men and women volunteered to join the armed forces. As enlistment between 1914 and the end of 1915 was voluntary, the individual had a certain amount of opportunity to influence which regiment/corps he joined. Although the individual's profession may have been taken into account, unless they were a specialist they would nearly always go into the infantry.

One of the most frequent misconceptions is that which regiment/corps an individual served in related to their place of domicile/enlistment and that they usually joined the local unit. The 'Pals' units, such as the 'Accrington Pals' (the 11th Battalion, East Lancashire) or the 'Civil Service Rifles' (the 15th Battalion, London Regiment), were in most cases made up of people from a given geographical area or occupation. However, if a man came from Carlisle, for example, it did not mean he would necessarily join a battalion of the Border Regiment. Depending upon the recruiting officer and his affiliations, the choice of the recruit or the needs of the Army, the man could end up in almost any regiment or corps.

There were, however, regional strengths with regard to recruiting, and there still are. Many men from Aberdeen joined the Gordon Highlanders, for example, while Nottingham was a strong area for recruiting men to join the King's Royal Rifle Corps.

Once conscription started in 1916 the needs of the Army were foremost when it came to the allocation of manpower, although specialists would usually be employed in appropriate units.

16.3 Age

The age of an individual can have an important bearing upon your research.

Many men who saw service in the late nineteenth century and who left the Army before 1914, went back into the Army at some time between 1914 and 1918. If a man was deemed fit enough to serve, and was under 60, the Army could find a use for him, especially if he was an old soldier.

Many men lied about their age to get into the Army; some boys were too young and added a few years to their age on enlistment, while some older men knocked a few years off—and then regretted it!

The maximum age for conscription was 56 years old, depending upon the personal circumstances of the individual.

The oldest known battle casualty in the British Army during the First World War was Henry Webber, who was 68 years old when he died in 1916.

16.4 Changing Units

Many people researching ancestors who served in the First World War have photographs of the same man, but showing him in different units (identified by different badges, for example). There are a number of reasons for these differences.

If a man became sick or was wounded during the war, it was not uncommon for him to be posted to a different battalion of the same regiment once he had recovered. As the needs of the Army dictated, so an individual could be transferred from one unit to another.

As the war progressed the manpower issues became more acute. In early 1918 the number of battalions in an Infantry Brigade was reduced from four to three. The manpower of the battalion reduced in these cases was either spread around the remaining battalions in the brigade—and in many cases this meant changing regiments—or was sent as reinforcements to battalions of their regiment, but in other brigades or divisions.

There were other reasons for an individual changing regiments or corps. For instance, the creation of the Machine Gun Corps in 1915 collected together machine gun trained personnel into a new corps and transferred them away from the regiments they had been serving in up until that time. If a man had served overseas as a machine gunner in his regiment in 1914 or 1915, his medal index card will be annotated with his original regiment and his number as well as Machine Gun Corps and his new number.

Many miners who joined the infantry in the early months of the war were later recruited into the Tunnelling Companies of the Royal Engineers and transferred to that corps permanently at a later date.

Many men who were wounded in the war, or who became sick during their service, were subsequently medically downgraded to a level where they were deemed not fit enough to serve in the infantry. Men such as these were frequently transferred to the Labour Corps and for the remainder of the war they worked moving equipment and ammunition, for example.

16.5   Researching Other Ranks

To start researching an ordinary soldier all that is needed is the name, but if you have already read the preceding parts of this chapter, you will know that to be effective in your research you will need more!

Although you can look at the records discussed in this book in almost any order, there are some things that can only be consulted if you have precise information. The following records need to be consulted to create the fullest picture of a man's career. Be aware that gathering information from some of these sources may be hindered by other gaps in your knowledge—for instance, not knowing exactly which units a person served in—and, perhaps more importantly, by the fact that the information may not have survived.

For a man who served overseas	For a man who did not serve overseas
1 Medal	Index Card
2 Record of Service	Record of Service
3 Unit War Diary	Unit War Diary (very few for home service)

You can search for a medal index card or a record of service with as little as the name, but you need the specific unit in order to locate a unit war diary in WO 95.

For a man who died in service
1   Check the Commonwealth War Graves Commission website
2   Check *Soldiers Died in The Great War*

If a man is buried in a CWGC grave or commemorated on a CWGC memorial, the entry on the website will give you the name, rank, number, unit and date of death, which you can then apply to the appropriate records. The CWGC does record dates of death after 11 November 1918.

Soldiers Died in the Great War will provide the name, rank, number, unit, date of death, place of enlistment and place of domicile. The data from *Soldiers Died in the Great War* can be applied to the records. *Soldiers Died in the Great War* only records 59 men who died after 11 November 1918.

Once you have obtained the information from the CWGC or *Soldiers Died in the Great War*, you should be able to approach the records in WO 363 and WO 364 with more confidence.

Eventually all of the records in WO 363 and WO 364 will be digitized and placed on *www.ancestry.co.uk*, where you will be able to search by as little as the name of a soldier. However, to make an effective search for a record of service at present, the order in which you search the records can be prioritized, depending upon the career of the soldier.

If a soldier died in service (especially overseas)

1   Check WO 363 (he should not be in WO 364)

If a soldier was medically discharged

1   Check WO 364
2   Check PIN 26
3   Check WO 363

If a soldier served and survived

1   Check WO 363
2   Check WO 364
3   Check PIN 26

There will always be exceptions to the rule, so although you may wish to follow the order of searching as described above, please look at all available records to eliminate them from your research and to satisfy any doubts you may have.

16.6   Regimental Numbers

The regimental number of an individual soldier is a very important piece of information that will help you in your research. However,

Fig.52 *Minute sheet from an officer's record, giving brief details about where he was to be trained as an officer and his subsequent appointment and postings.*
WO 339/63641

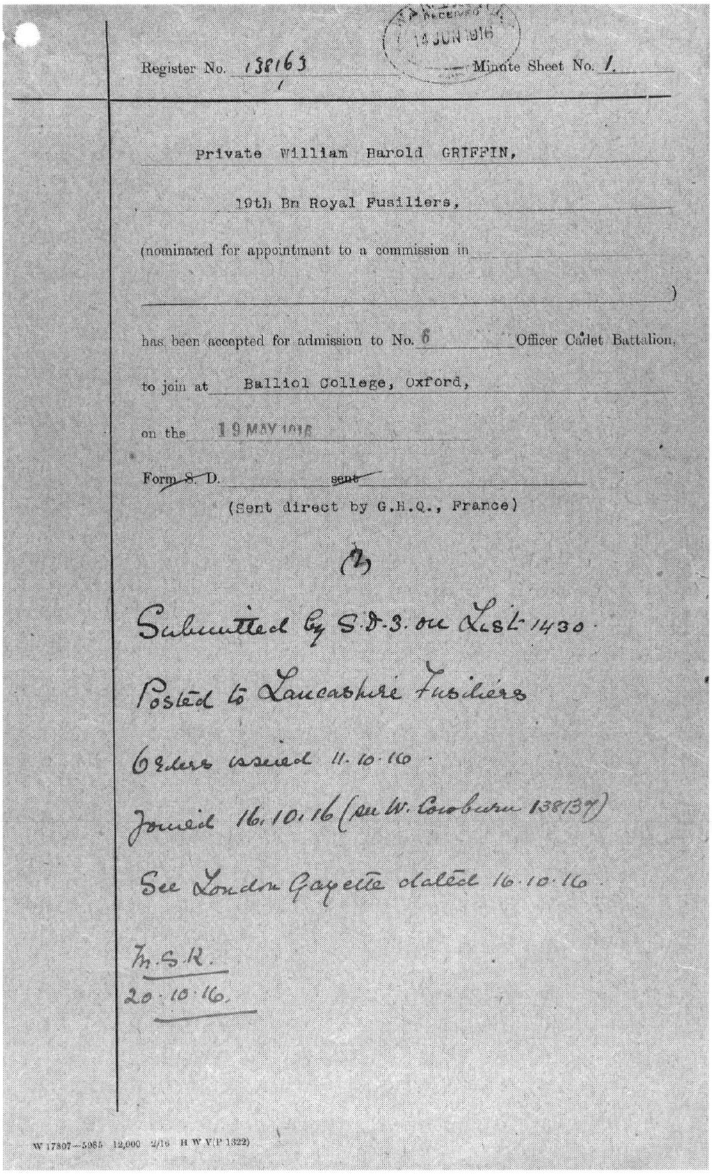
RECEIVED 14 JUN 1916

Register No. 138163 Minute Sheet No. 1.

Private William Harold GRIFFIN,

19th Bn Royal Fusiliers,

(nominated for appointment to a commission in ____________________)

has been accepted for admission to No. 6 Officer Cadet Battalion,

to join at Balliol College, Oxford,

on the 19 MAY 1916

~~Form S.~~ D. ~~sent~~

(Sent direct by G.H.Q., France)

(2)

Submitted by S.D.3. on List 1430.

Posted to Lancashire Fusiliers

Orders issued 11.10.16.

Joined 16.10.16 (see W. Cowburn 138137)

See London Gazette dated 16.10.16.

M.S.R.
20.10.16.

W 17807—5985 12,000 2/16 H W V(P 1322)

prior to August 1920 it was possible for more than one man to have the same number, as men were numbered by their regiment and not by the Army. Within regiments it was still possible for men to have the same number, but in most cases they would have been in different battalions.

A large number of prefixes and suffixes were used with regimental numbers, either to indicate a particular battalion, specialization or trade, for example.

The Army was renumbered during 1916 and 1917, and many of

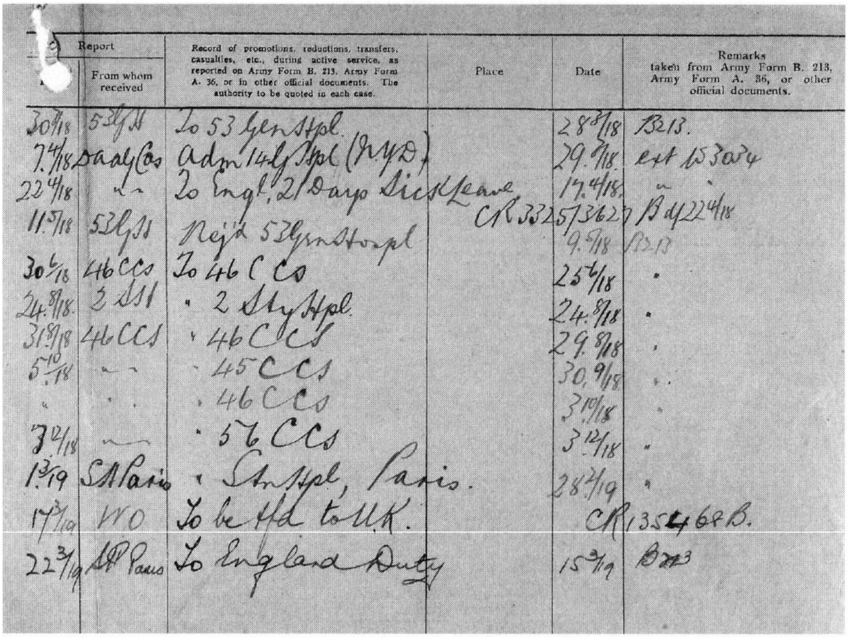

Fig. 53 *A detailed Army Form B 103 giving a full list of postings and movements.*

WO 399/6979

the Territorial Force soldiers were given new six-digit numbers. It is therefore possible to find old and new numbers for Territorial Force soldiers on their medal index cards if they served overseas before the end of 1915.

For a full explanation of regimental numbers in the First World War, the prefixes and suffixes and the numbers allocated to specific units, see *The Collector and Researcher's Guide to The Great War* by H. Williamson.

16.7   Researching an Officer

Although the number of officers commissioned between 1914 and 1918 was only 250,000, it is still possible to find two officers of the same name in the same regiment or corps. However, researching them is not as problematic as ordinary soldiers.

The first place to start the research for an officer is the *Army List*. The monthly *Army List* details all officers in the British Army for each month of the war. The *Army List* will tell you the regiment or corps an officer was commissioned into and the date of that commission. Once you have the unit, there are two ways to proceed. Either you can keyword search the Catalogue for WO 339 and WO 374 by using the surname and at least the first initial of the officer concerned. Or you can use WO 338, which is the index of the all important

Long Numbers, and apply the reference to wo 339 or wo 374 as appropriate (see chapter 2).

Officers who qualified for campaign medals may be found in the medal index cards in wo 372, but, unlike the other ranks, officers had to apply for their medals. If they did not apply for their medals, there will not be a medal index card.

The medal index cards for officers frequently do not show the forename(s) and consequently if you search for a card on DocumentsOnline you may have to search by surname and initial(s) only.

Officers who have hyphenated surnames can cause problems, simply because the Army frequently used the last part of their surname and any preceding parts as initials. As one might imagine, there are always variations to this, but you may wish to try searching by the last part of a hyphenated surname first and then add the other parts as appropriate.

16.8 RFC then RAF

Prior to the creation of the Royal Air Force (RAF), on 1 April 1918, the Royal Flying Corps (RFC) was a corps of the Army. Ordinary soldiers could join the RFC directly; officers usually transferred in from another regiment or corps.

If you know a man served in the RFC and then the RAF, but are unsure of his original regiment or corps, you may wish to try to find his RAF record of service and reverse-engineer his former service. The records of service of RAF officers are in the series AIR 76, arranged in alphabetical order, while the records of RAF airmen are in AIR 79, arranged by service number. Both sets of records in AIR 76 and AIR 79 will tell you the former regiment or corps of an individual prior to their service in the RFC.

16.9 Finding Unit War Diaries

Unit designations of the British Army are such that in order to find a unit war diary in wo 95 it may be necessary to restrict your research to ensure the correct result. The following guidance for the different parts of the army — infantry, cavalry, artillery, Army Service Corps, Royal Engineers and medical units—may help.

16.9.1 Infantry Regiments
A search for the Middlesex Regiment only will produce 48 results. In

Fig. 54 (facing)
*A piper of the 7th
Seaforth Highlanders
leads men of the 26th
Brigade back from
the trenches after the
attack on Longueval
on 14 July 1916 at
Battle of Bazentin
Ridge.*

order to get the correct diary, you need to specify the battalion. There are a number of caveats to bear in mind when searching for a specific battalion.

The regular battalions of a regiment were usually numbered 1 and 2 and can be found by searching for '1 AND Middlesex', for example. This search produces diaries for the following battalions: 1, 1/7, 1/8, 1/9, 1 Special Company and 1 Garrison Battalion.

The Territorial Force battalions of a regiment were usually numbered 1/8, 2/8 or 3/8, for example, so a search using '8 AND Middlesex' will produce results where 8 and Middlesex appear in the unit war diary description. The result for this search produces results for 1/8 and 3/8 battalions of the Middlesex Regiment only.

Terms such as 'Accrington' or 'Pals' are not used when describing unit war diaries, so it is necessary to know the exact regimental designation of such units in order to identify and order a unit war diary in WO 95. An incomplete list of 'Pals' battalions can be found at *www.en.wikipedia.org/wiki/List_of_Pals_battalions*. Further information about 'Pals' battalions can be found in *British Regiments 1914–1918* by E.A. James.

A number of very good guides about a number of the 'Pals' battalions have been published by Pen and Sword. According to the Pen and Sword website, *www.pen-and-sword.co.uk*, the following are currently in print: Accrington, Barnsley, Birmingham, Durham, Hull, Leeds, Liverpool, Manchester, Salford, Sheffield, Swansea and Wearside.

16.9.2 Cavalry

Finding a unit war diary for a cavalry regiment is not as complicated as the infantry. While you can search for the unit by the full name, it is safer to search by the type of regiment (Dragoons, Dragoon Guards, Lancers or Hussars) and by the numerical identity only.

16.9.3 Artillery

The Royal Artillery was further split into the Horse Artillery, Field Artillery and Garrison Artillery, with each section broken down into batteries and brigades, for example. The simplest way to locate an artillery unit war diary is to search using the battery or brigade numerical or alphabetical identity and the word art*. A search such as '233 AND art*' will produce the unit war diary for 233 Brigade, Royal Field Artillery in WO 95/2674.

16.9.4 Army Service Corps (ASC)

You should search for an Army Service Corps (ASC) unit war diary by the numerical identity of the company. However, the easiest way

to identify an ASC unit war diary is to consult *Army Service Corps 1902–1918* by M. Young, as it contains a full list of the diaries in WO 95 and is arranged by unit. A copy of the book is available in the National Archives Library.

16.9.5 *Royal Engineers (RE)*

Unit war diaries for the Royal Engineers (RE) are mostly described by their company number and should be searched for that way. A number of specialized units, such as the tunnelling companies, survey units and special (gas) companies, can be searched for by using 'tunnel*', 'survey*' or 'special' as appropriate.

16.9.6 *Medical Units*

General Hospitals, Field Ambulances and Casualty Clearing Stations all had numerical parts to their identities and these should be used to locate appropriate war diaries in WO 95. Combined terms searches such as '2 AND cas*' will find the unit war diary for 2 Casualty Clearing Station in WO 95/250. The same search will also produce results for three other unit war diaries where the search terms were also part of the unit descriptions.

16.10 Ranks

Irrespective of which regiment or corps an officer was in, the ranks they used were always the same. The officer at the bottom of the tree was second lieutenant and the man at the top a field marshal. The same is not to be said for other ranks. Different regiment and corps used different terms for their privates and non-commissioned officers. The following are a few examples where the rank was the same:

> private, rifleman, trooper, sapper, gunner, pioneer

Further information about the different army ranks used in the First World War can be found in *The Collector and Researcher's Guide to The Great War* by H. Williamson.

16.11 Medal Index Card Remarks Box

In the remarks box of many medal index cards can be found additional information about an individual and these include dates of commissioning, discharge, demobilization or death. Many other annotations in the remarks box include such things as 'KR 392 (xvi)' and 'Class Z', for example.

KR 392 (xvi) refers to King's Regulations paragraph 329 article xvi, which means the individual was discharged on account of sickness or wounds. A copy of King's Regulations is available on the open shelves in the Open Reading Room.

'Class Z' refers to men who were discharged to Class Z of the Army Reserve, and in basic terms meant that an individual was demobilized but placed on the reserve subject to recall if the Army needed them. Class Z was only used for men who joined the army during the First World War, and did not include pre-war Regular Army soldiers or member of the pre-war Territorial Force.

CALDERDALE LIBRARIES

APPENDIX 1

Regimental Order of Precedence

The following order of precedence is applicable to the First World War period but it does represent information that may be needed to use many of the records for the 1914–20 period. The order is based on the date specific units were originally founded. The number at the end of each infantry regiment, starting with the Royal Scots, is the original numerical identity of the unit prior to 1881 and is the number used to identify the regiment in the index of officers' Long Numbers in wo 338.

1 Life Guards
2 Life Guards
Royal Horse Guards
Household Battalion
Royal Horse Artillery
1 King's Dragoon Guards
2 Dragoon Guards (Queen's Bays)
3 (Prince of Wales's) Dragoon Guards
4 (Royal Irish) Dragoon Guards
5 (Princess Charlotte of Wales's) Dragoon Guards
6 Dragoon Guards (Carabiniers)
7 (The Princess Royal's) Dragoon Guards
1 (Royal) Dragoons
2 Dragoons (Royal Scots Greys)
3 (King's Own) Hussars
4 (The Queen's Own) Hussars
5 (Royal Irish) Lancers
6 (Inniskilling) Dragoons
7 (Queen's Own) Hussars
8 The King's Royal Irish) Hussars
9 (Queen's Royal) Lancers
10 (The Prince of Wales's Own) Hussars
11 Prince Albert's Own) Hussars
12 (The Prince of Wales's Royal) Lancers
13 Hussars
14 (King's) Hussars
15 (King's) Hussars
16 (The Queen's) Lancers
17 Lancers (Duke of Cambridge's Own)
18 Hussars
19 Hussars
20 Hussars
21 (Empress of India's) Lancers

The Yeomanry Regiments (as follows)
  Royal Wiltshire

Warwickshire
Yorkshire Hussars
Sherwood Rangers
Staffordshire
Shropshire
Ayrshire
Cheshire
Yorkshire Dragoons
Leicestershire
North Somerset
Duke of Lancaster's Own
Lanarkshire
Northumberland
South Notts Hussars
Denbighshire
Westmoreland and Cumberland
Pembroke
Royal East Kent
Hampshire
Buckinghamshire
Derbyshire
Dorset
Gloucestershire
Herts
Bucks
1st County of London (Middlesex Hussars)
Royal 1st Devon
Suffolk
Royal North Devon
Worcestershire
West Kent
West Somerset
Oxfordshire
Montgomeryshire
Lothian and Border Horse
Lanarkshire (Glasgow)
Lancashire Hussars
Surrey
Fife and Forfar
Norfolk
Sussex
Glamorgan
Welsh Horse
Lincolnshire
City of London (Rough Riders)
2nd County of London (Westminster Dragoons)
3rd County of London (Sharpshooters)
Bedfordshire
Essex

Northamptonshire
East Riding of Yorkshire
1st Lovat's Scouts
2nd Lovat's Scouts
Scottish Horse

Royal Artillery
Royal Field Artillery
Royal Engineers
Royal Flying Corps
Grenadier Guards
Coldstream Guards
Scots Guards
Irish Guards
Welsh Guards
Royal Scots (Lothian) 1
Queen's (Royal West Surrey) 2
Buffs (East Kent) 3
King's Own (Royal Lancaster) 4
Northumberland Fusiliers 5
Royal Warwickshire 6
Royal Fusiliers (City of London) 7
The King's (Liverpool) 8
Norfolk 9
Lincolnshire 10
Devonshire 11
Suffolk 12
Prince Albert's (Somerset Light Infantry) 13
Prince of Wales's Own (East Yorkshire) 14
East Yorkshire 15
Bedfordshire 16
Leicestershire 17
Royal Irish 18
Alexandra, Princess of Wales's (Yorkshire) 19
Lancashire Fusiliers 20
Royal Scots Fusiliers 21
Cheshire 22
Royal Welsh Fusiliers 23
South Wales Borderers 24
King's Own Scottish Borderers 25
Cameronians (Scottish Rifles) 26
Royal Inniskilling Fusiliers 27
Gloucestershire 28
Worcestershire 29
East Lancashire 30
East Surrey 31
Duke of Cornwall's Light Infantry 32
Duke of Wellington's (West Riding) 33
Border 34
Royal Sussex 35
Hampshire 37
South Staffordshire 38
Dorsetshire 39
Prince of Wales's Volunteers (South Lancashire) 40

Welsh 41
Black Watch (Royal Highlanders) 42
Oxfordshire and Buckinghamshire Light Infantry 43
Essex 44
Sherwood Foresters (Nottinghamshire and
    Derbyshire) 45
Loyal North Lancashire 47
Northamptonshire 48
Princess Charlotte of Wales's (Royal Berkshire) 49
Queen's Own (Royal West Kent) 50
King's Own (Yorkshire Light Infantry) 51
King's (Shropshire Light Infantry) 53
Duke of Cambridge's Own (Middlesex) 57
King's Royal Rifle Corps 60
Duke of Edinburgh's (Wiltshire) 62
Manchester 63
Prince of Wales's (North Staffordshire) 64
York and Lancaster 65
Durham Light Infantry 68
Highland Light Infantry 71
Seaforth Highlanders (Ross-shire Buffs, The Duke
    of Albany's) 72
Gordon Highlanders 75
Queen's Own Cameron Highlanders 79
Royal Irish Rifles 83
Princess Victoria's (Royal Irish Fusiliers) 87
Connaught Rangers 88
Princess Louise's (Argyll and Sutherland
    Highlanders) 91
Prince of Wales's Leinster (Royal Canadians) 100
Royal Munster Fusiliers 101
Royal Dublin Fusiliers 102
Rifle Brigade
Royal Army Chaplains Department
Army Service Corps
Royal Army Medical Corps
Army Ordnance Corps
Army Veterinary Corps
Machine Gun Corps
Royal Tank Corps
Labour Corps
Honourable Artillery Company
Monmouthshire Regiment
Cambridgeshire Regiment
London Regiment
Hertfordshire Regiment
Northern Cyclist Battalion
Highland Cyclist Battalion
Kent Cyclist Battalion
Huntingdon Cyclist Battalion

This order of precedence is based on the Army List
of August 1914, to which have been added a
number of units created between 1914 and 1918.

APPENDIX 2

Regional Record Offices

All Army record offices administering records of service and gathering data for the creation of the First World War campaign medal rolls were given a code letter. These letters were used at the beginning of the Army Medal Office medal roll references; details are given below.

Code	Record Office
A	Cork
B	Dublin
C	Exeter
CC	Cavalry Canterbury
CY	Cavalry York
D	Hamilton
E	Hounslow
F	Lichfield
G	Perth
H	Preston
J	Shrewsbury
K	Warley
L	Warwick
M	Winchester
O	York
TP	London

The following regiment–to–record office allocation list may help to interpret the medal rolls, and also to show which regiment's records were administered by which office.

Record Office Code	Regiments
A	Royal Irish
	Connaught Rangers
	Royal Munster Fusiliers
	Leinster
B	Royal Dublin Fusiliers
	Royal Inniskilling Fusiliers
	Royal Irish Fusiliers
	Royal Irish Rifles
C	Duke of Cornwall's Light Infantry
	Wiltshire
	Hampshire
	Dorset
	Somerset Light Infantry
	Devon
CC	Bedfordshire Yeomanry
	Berkshire Yeomanry
	City of London Yeomanry
	2nd County of London Yeomanry
	Derbyshire Yeomanry
	Duke of Lancaster's Own
	East Riding of Yorkshire
	Essex Yeomanry
	Fire and Forfar Yeomanry
	Glamorgan Yeomanry
	Hampshire Yeomanry
	Herts Yeomanry
	Lanarkshre Yeomanry
	Lincolnshire Yeomanry
	Lothian and Border Horse
	Lovat's Scouts
	Montgomeryshire Yeomanry
	Norfolk Yeomanry
	Northampton Yeomanry
	North Somerset Yeomanry
	Queen's Own Glasgow
	Scottish Horse
	Shropshire Yeomanry
	Surrey Yeomanry
	Sussex Yeomanry
	Yorkshire Dragoons
CY	Ayrshire Yeomanry
	Buckinghamshire Yeomanry
	Cheshire Yeomanry
	1st County of London Yeomanry
	3rd County of London Yeomanry
	Denbighshire Yeomanry
	Gloucester Yeomanry
	Lancashire Hussars
	Leicester Yeomanry
	Northumberland Yeomanry
	Nottinghamshire Yeomanry
	Oxfordshire Yeomanry
	Pembroke Yeomanry
	1st Royal Devon Yeomanry
	Royal East Kent
	Royal North Devon Yeomanry

Royal Wiltshire Yeomanry
South Notts Hussars
Staffordshire Yeomanry
Suffolk Yeomanry
Warwick Yeomanry
West Kent Yeomanry
Westmoreland and Cumberland Yeomanry
West Somerset Yeomanry
Worcestershire Yeomanry
Yorkshire Hussars

D   Royal Scots
Royal Scots Fusiliers
Scottish Rifles (Cameronians)
Highland Light Infantry
King's Own Scottish Borderers

E   Queen's Royal West Surrey
Middlesex
East Surrey
Royal Sussex
East Kent (Buffs)
Royal West Kent
Cyclist Corps

F   South Staffordshire
North Staffordshire
Notts and Derby (Sherwood Foresters)
Leicester
Lincoln

G   Gordon Highlanders
Royal Highlanders (Black Watch)
Cameron Highlanders
Seaforth Highlanders
Argyll and Sutherland Highlanders

H   Lancashire Fusiliers
East Lancashire
Border
Manchester
Loyal North Lancashire
Liverpool (King's)
King's Own (Royal Lancaster)

J   South Wales Borderers
King's Shropshire Light Infantry
South Lancashire
Welsh
Cheshire
Royal Welsh Fusiliers
Monmouth

K   Northamptonshire
Norfolk
Suffolk
Cambridge
Herefordshire
Essex
Bedfordshire

L   Gloucestershire
Worcestershire
Royal Warwickshire
Berkshire
Oxfordshire and Buckinghamshire Light Infantry

M   King's Royal Rifle Corps
Rifle Brigade

O   Yorkshire
East Yorkshire
Durham Light Infantry
Northumberland Fusiliers
Duke of Wellington's (West Riding)
York and Lancaster
King's Own Yorkshire Light Infantry
West Yorkshire

TP   London
Royal Fusiliers
Royal Defence Corps
Honourable Artillery Company

The records of nurses and officers were administered at the War Office, and the references for their medal rolls are prefixed 'Nurses' and 'Off' respectively.

The record offices for the Guards and Corps of the British Army were in a number of different locations from the infantry and cavalry record offices. The prefixes used on the medal rolls for the Guards and Corps are mostly self-explanatory.

A fuller list of record office and pay office allocations can be found on pages 379–87 of *The Collector and Researcher's Guide to The Great War* by H. Williamson (see p.156).

APPENDIX 3

Post-First World War Records of Service

The records of service of other ranks who were discharged after 1920 — and officers who served at any point after 31 March 1922 — are still with the Ministry of Defence. Only the next of kin can obtain further information from the MOD until such time as the records are transferred to The National Archives.

For further information contact:

Army Personnel Centre
Historical Disclosures
Mail Point 555
Kentigern House
65 Brown Street
Glasgow
G2 8EX
Tel: 0845 6009663

FURTHER READING AND WEBSITES

Books

P.E. Abbott and J.M.A. Tamplin, *British Gallantry Awards* (Nimrod Dix, 1981)

The Army List

Military Museums in The UK (Army Museums Ogilby Trust, 2006)

Battleground Europe series. various authors (Leo Cooper, 1994–2001)

A.F. Becke, *History of The Great War: Orders of Battle* (HMSO, 1937–45)

I.F.W. Beckett, *Home Front 1914–1918: How Britain Survived the Great War* (National Archives, 2006)

I.F.W. Beckett, *The First World War: the Essential Guide to Sources in the UK National Archives* (PRO, 2002)

I.F.W. Beckett and K. Simpson, *A Nation in Arms: A Social Study of the British Army in the First World War* (Tom Donovan, 1990)

E.W. Bell, ed., *Soldiers Killed on the First Day of the Somme* (1977)

A. Bevan, *Tracing Your Ancestors in the National Archives* (7th edition, National Archives, 2006)

D. Birch, J. Hayward and R. Bishop, *British Battles and Medals* (Spink, 2006)

J.M. Bourne, *Who's Who in World War One* (Routledge, 2001)

G. Corrigan, *Sepoys in the Trenches: The Indian Corps on the Western Front 1914–1915* (Spellmount, 1999)

Cox and Co., *List of Officers taken prisoner in the Various Theatres of War between August 1914 and November 1918*

General O'Moore Creagh and E.M. Humphris, *The Distinguished Service Order 1886–1923* (Hayward, 1988)

F. Davies and G. Maddocks, *Bloody Red Tabs* (Leo Cooper, 1995)

J.C. Dunn, *The War the Infantry Knew* (Cardinal, 1989)

W. Ellsworth-Jones, *We Will Not Fight: The Untold Story of World War One's Conscientious Objectors* (Aurum, 2008)

A. Farrington, *Guide to the Records of the India Office Military Department* (London, 1982)

N. Holding, *World War I Army Ancestry* (FFHS, 1997)

N. Holding, *More Sources of World War I Army Ancestry* (FFHS, 1997)

Honours and Awards Indian Army 1914–1921 (Hayward, n.d.)

The Indian Army List

E.A. James, *British Regiments 1914–1918* (Naval and Military Press, 1993)

S.B. and D.B. Jarvis, *Cross of Sacrifice*, vols I–V (Roberts and Naval and Military Press, 1988–2000)

The London Gazette

Y. McEwen, *It's a Long Way to Tipperary: British and Irish Nurses in the Great War* (Cualann Press, 2006)

M. McGregor, *Officers of the Durham Light Infantry* (McGregor, 1989)

I. McInnes, *Meritorious Service Medal. The Immediate Awards 1916–1928* (Jade, 1988)

I. McInnes and J.V. Webb, *A Contemptible Little Flying Corps* (London Stamp Exchange, 1991)

M. Middlebrook, *Your Country Needs You* (Leo Cooper, 2000)

Military Museums in the UK (Army Museums Ogilby Trust, 2007)

National Roll of Honour 1914–1918

Officers Died in the Great War (HMSO, 1922)

The Official History (HMSO, various dates up to 1947)

G. Oram, *Death Sentences Passed by Military Courts of the British Army 1914–1920* (Francis Boutle, 1998)

J. Putkowski and J. Sykes, *Shot at Dawn* (Leo Cooper, 1998)

J. Putkowski, *British Army Mutineers 1914–1922* (Francis Boutle, 1999)

P. Simkins, *Kitchener's Army* (Manchester University Press, 1990)

A. Simpson, *Directing Operations: British Corps Command on The Western Front 1914–1918* (Spellmount, 2006)

Soldiers Died in the Great War (HMSO, 1922)

W. Spencer, *Air Force Records: A Guide for Family Historians* (TNA, 2008)

W. Spencer, *Army Records: A Guide for Family Historians* (TNA, 2008)

W. Spencer, *Medals: the Researcher's Guide* (TNA, 2008)

W. Spencer, *Records of the Militia and Volunteer Forces 1757–1945* (PRO, 1997)

Statistics of British Military Effort (HMSO, 1922)

I. Swinnerton, *Identifying Your World War I Soldier from Badges and Photographs* (FFHS, 2001)

R.W. Walker, *To What End Did They Die: Officers Who Died at Gallipoli* (1980)

R.W. Walker, *Recipients of the Distinguished Conduct Medal 1914–1920* (Midland Medals, 1980)

R.W. Walker and C. Buckland, *Citations of the Distinguished Conduct Medal 1914–1920* (Naval and Military Press, 2007)

S. Walker, *Forgotten Soldiers: The Irishmen Shot at Dawn* (Gill and Macmillan, 2007)

R. Westlake, *British Battalions at Gallipoli* (Leo Cooper, 1996)

R. Westlake, *British Battalions in Belgium and France 1914* (Leo Cooper, 1997)

R. Westlake, *British Battalions on the Somme* (Leo Cooper, 1994)

R. Westlake, *British Battalions on the Western Front January–June 1915* (Leo Cooper, 2000)

R. Westlake, *Kitchener's Army* (Spellmount, 1998)

I.R. Whitehead, *Doctors in the Great War* (Leo Cooper, 1999)

H. Williamson, *The Collector and Researcher's Guide to The Great War* (privately published, 2003)

M. Young, *Army Service Corps 1902–1918* (Pen and Sword, 2000)

Websites

www.nationalarchives.gov.uk
www.gazettes-online.co.uk
www.1914-1918.net
www.iwm.org.uk
www.bl.uk
www.mod.uk
www.armymuseums.org.uk
www.pals.org.uk/pals_e.htm